EVERYDAY MAGIC: CHILD LANGUAGES IN CANADIAN LITERATURE

Everyday Magic,

Child Languages
in Canadian Literature

(Laurie) Ricou, Laurence

The University of British Columbia Press
Vancouver 1987

EVERYDAY MAGIC: CHILD LANGUAGES IN CANADIAN LITERATURE

The University of British Columbia Press 1987

This book has been published with the help of a grant from the Canadian Federation for the Humanities, using funds provided by the Social Sciences and Humanities Research Council of Canada.

Canadian Cataloguing in Publication Data

Ricou, Laurence, 1944-
Everyday Magic

Includes index.
ISBN 0-7748-0277-4
1. Canadian literature (English) — 20th century — History and criticism.* 2. Children in literature. 3. Children — Language.
I. Title.
PS8103.C5R53 1987   C810'.9'352054
PR9185.6.C5R53 1987   C87-091206-2

International Standard Book Number 0-7748-0277-4

Printed in Canada

for Marc and Liane

CONTENTS

PREFACE

Intersections in Surprise

Just a few days before I was to send this manuscript to the press I received from Robert Kroetsch his book of poems *Advice to My Friends*. His advice to me, which through a series of accidents I had never heard before, was "Let the surprise surprise you."[1] It must be in the nature of such advice to be ignored, but Kroetsch's urging is the perfect preface to this book. Child language is hardly a subject whose appeal is limited to theorists, Ph.D's, and researchers behind one-way mirrors. Child language is surprising because everybody is an expert on the subject. All parents study their children's language carefully, if undeliberately, and every family has its precious memories of the unique verbal improvisations of childhood. My aunt (we call her "Dee," the name we used before we could say Aunt Phyl) still reminds me that I always called screwdrivers 'skewdabby.' But you don't need to be a parent to be mesmerized by this distinctive language, as I was reminded while watching the fireworks at Vancouver's annual Sea Festival. Dozens of people around me were more delighted, more amused, by a small girl's running commentary than by the spectacle itself: one formation she called "Smarties"; 'I can't keep myself from saying oooh, and then aaah,' she marvelled to her mother. Her surprise surprised us.

If the language of children is so widely interesting, it might hold a special fascination for imaginative writers who struggle every day with the mysteries of language, and the frustrating possibilities of verbal expression. This book makes the different—yet twinned—subjects of children and language its centre of attention; this is a study of children in literature (a subject not to be confused with children's literature) as shaped by the study of child language. Where, and to what extent, do the distinctive features of child language described by psycholinguists intersect with the written language which the writer uses to suggest not only child *language*, but also the way a child sees and organizes an understanding of the world? In my title I use the term "child languages," in the plural, to suggest the multiple answers to this question, and to remind the reader that child language, more empirically defined, is a continuing point of reference. The book is, in sum, a meditation on the ways that the child surprises the adult artist and on the surprising speech of early childhood.

This is a study of Canadian literature, because Canadian literature is my specialty. It is not, however, an argument that children are particularly prominent in Canadian literature. I am convinced that Canadian literature offers the wide range of rich and complex texts to support a study which I hope will have implications for understanding a general literary problem/challenge hardly restricted to Canadian writing. The book proposes analogies with Wordsworth and Dylan Thomas, with Proust and Dickens, but it finds its principal subject in the inherent interest of, for example, the Piagetian scheme that W.O. Mitchell seems to adopt in *Who Has Seen the Wind*, the obsession with similes in Ernest Buckler, the variations on the *Bildungsroman* in Margaret Laurence and Alice Munro, and the persistent experiments with pre-symbolic language in bill bissett. It should be clear from this list that I try to avoid imposing one thesis on these very different writers, but rather try to illuminate the particular literary languages appropriate to each writer's subject. Many scholars and critics have written well on the images of childhood in literature; until 1984 no one had written more than a few sentences on the specific features of language appropriate to the child as subject.

As with any study that develops over a long period (I had an inkling of the subject in 1973 and began writing in 1976), both study and subject kept slipping and changing under my feet as I was writing. When I began, a study focusing on Canadian literature in a more interdisciplinary way seemed essential—now I would rather be writing a more comparative study. But one of the pleasures a university teacher enjoys in extra measure is the sense of never being finished, of constantly encountering some new idea, some fugitive poem, some unread scrap of Aristotle or some comment by a student that will disturb assumptions and reveal something unexpected. I can only hope that this study is sufficiently unique to disturb someone else's assumptions, to suggest an approach to other texts through the perspective of child language.

Also, during the gestation of this study, theory—which is to say structuralist and post-structuralist, semiotic theory, with its European roots—made its massive impact on North American literary scholarship. It is in part accidental that much of this theory, from Roman Jakobson on metonymy to Julia Kristeva on the infant language in all language, has its roots in the psycholinguistic study of child language. But as the authors and the referents, and even the words themselves, disappeared as I read various theoretical formulations, I kept coming back to questions of how does this writer do this, and does that doing have links, or can it be more fully understood by what I am learning about the unique features of child language. Everyone knows about the uniqueness of a child's world view. What, I wanted to know, if the theory and the language would sit still for a minute, was how the propositions about the uniqueness of child language might be tied into this cultural and literary commonplace.

This book pays a good deal of attention to the results of scientific method and empirical observation. But while I salute my colleagues in psycholinguistics—both those cited and the many who have contributed indirectly—I can lay little claim to their methods. Indeed, I expect my comments sometimes would prompt them to use the label "sentimental." But I cannot imagine writing a book on these subjects without yielding, at least on occasion, to a dumbfounded wonder at the unconscious poetry of child's speech and its poetic remaking in fiction, drama, and poems for adults. It's just because it's so everyday, that child language surprises us with magic.

ACKNOWLEDGEMENTS

Many colleagues generously read portions of this book in manuscript. My thanks for advice to my colleagues at the University of British Columbia: Jane Flick, Carole Gerson, Sherrill Grace, Eva-Marie Kröller, and Bill New. I am also grateful for critical comments to Helen Hoy, University of Lethbridge; Gerald Noonan, Sir Wilfrid Laurier University, and Alan Young, Acadia University. Many hours of talk with Roger Barnsley, then in the Department of Psychology, University of Lethbridge, and now at St. Mary's University, got me started reading in child language and gave a strong, continuing impetus to this study.

During a sabbatical year in 1982-83 I was fortunate to meet several fine scholars who responded generously and at length to my often naïve questions: Anne Sinclair and her colleagues at the University of Geneva; Els Oksaar and Jorgen Meisel of the University of Hamburg; Sven Strömquist of the University of Gothenburg; Natalie Waterson and her graduate student Vania Lins Eyre at the University of London; and Alison Elliot, Edinburgh University. Carol Thew, of the Faculty of Education, University of British Columbia, introduced me to this international network with an invitation to the Second International Congress for the Study of Child Language, Vancouver, August 1981. The research and travel was supported by grants from the University of Lethbridge, the University of British Columbia, and especially by two precious leave fellowships from the Social Sciences and Humanities Research Council of Canada. I am also grateful to the SSHRCC for funding the generous grant in aid of publication provided by the Canadian Federation for the Humanities.

Mary Jane Hurst, now at Texas Tech University, organized a session on "Child Language in Literature" at the 1984 MLA convention, thus giving me my first opportunity to meet other people working on the subject I had set myself. One of the contributors, Naomi Sokoloff, from the University of Washington, has been helpful in exchanging copies of her varied work on child language in Jewish-American literature. Hurst's own doctoral dissertation for the University of Maryland, "The Voice of the Child in Nineteenth-Century American Literature: Linguistic Approaches to Fictional Child Language," is an important source for anyone interested in child language in literature. Thomas Tausky, University of Western Ontario, shared with me his article on autobiographies of childhood, while it was still in manuscript.

Sheila Redel was my cheerful research assistant in the earliest stages of the project. Doreen Todhunter and Tom Friedman were both speedy and careful in entering the manuscript on the word processor. Treva Ricou originally typed the entire manuscript on a *supermarché* electric whose carriage would not slide. But that is only the most obvious contribution of a partner who shares this book in unnumbered ways.

It has been a pleasure to work again with the people at UBC Press: my particular thanks to Jim Anderson for his support, and to Jane Fredeman for her interest in the project over many years. I could not have wished for a better editor than Jean Wilson, who read the manuscript meticulously and sympathetically.

Parts of this book originally appeared, often in very different form, as follows: "Notes on Language and Learning in *Who Has Seen the Wind,*" *Canadian Children's Literature* 10 (1977-78): 3-17; "David Canaan and Buckler's Style in *The Mountain and the Valley,*" *Dalhousie Review:* 57.4 (Winter 1977-78): 684-96; "The Naïve Eye in the Poetry of Dorothy Livesay, P. K. Page, and Miriam Waddington," *Voices from Distant Lands: Poetry in the Commonwealth,* eds. Konrad Gross and Wolfgang Klooss (Würzburg: Königshausen and Neumann, 1983), pp. 108-14; "Emily Carr and the Language of Small," *Canada: The Verbal Creation/La Creazione Verbale,* ed. Alfredo Rizzardi (Abano: Piovan Editore, 1985), pp. 199-219.

. . . odd sounds in my throat
strange vocal doodles
as my adam's apple bobs
up and down like water coming
deep down in an old wooden pump
that sounds something like "guaý-au-goú"
a memory summoned from childhood
when for other kids
it was everyday magic
that made things happen
and then unhappen

Al Purdy, "Kikastan Communications"
NORTH OF SUMMER: POEMS FROM BAFFIN ISLAND
(Toronto: McClelland & Stewart, 1967), p. 67

& that was when we were almost simple, simply almost children,
or barely out of it, our simplicity we kept, a long time.
                                        . . .
Does he see lion when he says "the raahr" is
coming to get me?

Daphne Marlatt, "Broke,"
SELECTED WRITING: NET WORK
(Vancouver: Talonbooks, 1980), p. 88.

1

The "As If" of the Child's World: An Introduction to Child Language and the Child in Literature

Without language, the world would remain one continuous blob of colours and shapes, inseparable and indistinguishable. With language it becomes classifiable and ordered and apprehendable. Children seem to know this instinctively. They want to know the names of things, not out of idle curiosity, but because the names have for them magical properties. By naming the object, by chanting the name over and over again, by skipping about the object while repeating its name, the object becomes imaginatively penetrated, delineated, possessed.

James E. Miller Jr., WORD, SELF, REALITY

To keep the rhythms, the language "right," i.e. consistent with what a child would say or at least to create the "as if" of the child's world, was very difficult technically.

Theodore Roethke, "Open Letter"

The speed with which children accomplish the complex process of language acquisition is particularly impressive. Ten linguists working full time for 10 years to analyze the structure of the English language could not program a computer with the ability for language acquired by an average child in the first 10 or even five years of life.

Breyne Arlene Moskowitz, "The Acquisition of Language"

Through these three comments, differing in tone from the nostalgic to the deliberative to the analytical, runs a common fascination with the magic of child language. In the web of this fascination, connecting literary critic, poet, and psycholinguist, is tangled the subject of this book. The term "child language" has come to describe the unique spoken language that is the subject of so much empirical research;[1] making the term plural, child languages, is my abbreviated way of designating the many written interpretations of the child's perspective in literature. The intersection of child languages and writers' various grammars of childhood is my territory in this book. In appropriating the phrase "child language" from one discipline to designate a variety of discourses in another discipline, I intend that each mention of the term, from subtitle to summary, will embrace or hint at the intersections. Each writer's child language has different features—from the imagery of light and the rhapsodic lists in Thomas Traherne, to the shifted parts of speech in e. e. cummings. Child languages are plural: different writers, in different cultures, in different periods will use different methods to write the child's point of view.

To make this vast subject manageable, I take my primary examples of the writers' various grammars of childhood from the field I know best, modern English-Canadian literature. But I hope the term child languages is also a reminder of a language shared by all children, and, thus, will interest readers of other literatures as well.

An American poet, for example, makes one of the most succinct summaries of the artist's difficulty with wording the perception of the child. Theodore Roethke's comments on "The Flight," the first in the five-poem narrative sequence "The Lost Son," describe the writer's problem with children:

> ["The Flight"] is written entirely from the viewpoint of a very small child: all interior drama; no comment; no interpretation. To keep the rhythms, the language "right," i.e. consistent with what a child would say or at least to create the "as if" of the child's world, was very difficult technically. I don't believe anyone else has been foolish enough to attempt a tragedy in this particular way. The rhythms are very slow; there is no cutesy prattle; it is not a suite in goo-goo.[2]

Writing from the viewpoint of a small child, that is the pre-adolescent and, especially, the pre-school child, poses great technical difficulties. To exclude interpretation or comment sustains the illusion of a child's perspective. Using a language entirely "consistent with what a child would say" achieves a crucial distancing, but in that direction lies the danger of an absurd and boring "suite in goo-goo." The writer, it seems, must use enough child's language to give a consistent feel of what the child would say, yet exploit fully his mature technical resources to suggest the complexity of the child's mind.

"The Flight," for example, describes a child's "terrified running away";[3] it depends on language which seems "right" for a small child: the barely articulate simplicity of "This is my hard time" with its unattached pronoun and vague predication; the clamouring onomatopoeia"kingdom of bang and blab"; the playground metaphor of the leaves sticking out their tongues; or the monosyllabic trimeters of the nursery rhymes which end the poem:

> Is it soft like a mouse?
> Can it wrinkle its nose?
> Could it come in the house
> On the tips of its toes?

In these questions, according to Roethke, the child is chasing some half-apprehended "clue to existence from the sub-human." The psychic drama is plausibly childlike when expressed in a flow of images: from "dark hollows" through "wind," "moon," "eel" and "salt," to "sea." But technical difficulties intrude in the second stanza:

> Fished in an old wound,
> The soft pond of repose;
> Nothing nibbled my line,
> Not even the minnows came.[4]

By Roethke's own criterion of proximity to what a child would say, the first two of these lines, particularly, seem an uneasy imposition. They may be effective in evoking some aspect of the child's unconscious, but their remoteness from the vocabulary, syntax, and semantics of child language interrupts our sense of a small child's viewpoint.

Of course, the limits of critical interpretation are also evident. We do not know that the child's head would *not* be filled by the complex of thoughts and images floating in the soft pond of repose. Linguists always distinguish between children's performance and competence, and generally conclude that understanding exceeds articulation. We have little empirical evidence, and therefore scant understanding of the ideas informed by language, or unarticulated. They might be approached through a more Freudian or Jungian analysis than this book attempts. What interests me rather is the critical direction implied in Roethke's comment. Effective realization of the child's perspective depends, he suggests, either on using child language, or at least on finding some connection between that language and the " 'as if' of a child's world."

Each of the four features of "The Flight" which I have initially identified as "right" for the child raises its own questions about this connection between mature literary technique and child language. In exploring these connections I have had to keep in mind the claims of two disciplines. To the literary critic, and that perspective is of course primary for me, there are as many grammars of childhood as there are imaginative, independent interpretations of children by accomplished artists (many of whom have, presumably, never heard of formal studies of child language). The psycholinguist is more inclined to think of one universal child language, whose distinguishing structures can be described in great detail. Noam Chomsky's theories of linguistic structure have in the past three decades stimulated enormous interest in identification of the universals of language acquisition, and in empirical study of how children talk. But the Chomskyean paradigm has also been profoundly criticized.[5] Such debate—as in any academic discipline—will often seem intimidatingly rarefied and specific to a layperson. I am impressed that within the field of psycholinguistics there are profound theoretical divisions—between Chomsky's and Piaget's conception of the Language Acquisition Device, for instance. Even quite limited reading in the empirical literature will reveal many different child languages—determined by age, social class, context (school, playground and home), culture (multilingual or monolingual); or described by means of vocabulary, grammatical structures, or sociolinguistically by communicative competence. In this study my concern is not to resolve differing views in a field to which I am a visitor. A proposition about child language, even if it is empirically flawed, may have a powerful hold as a fiction. That child languages are plural is part of my argument about literature. That a particular description of child language might correspond to, or extend, what the layman—and writer—understands, consciously or unconsciously, about how a child speaks is central to my procedure. In the face of my own limitations I have tried to stay alert to the general characteristics and particular features of child language that could provide a vocabulary (with its inherent insight) for discussing the writer's difficulty with the distinctly different perception of the child's mind.

Our most complete evidence for the workings of that mind is its language. What is distinctive about child language? Obviously, and primarily, it is language in the *process of being learned*, unlike adult language, where only the knowledge of semantics is likely to change in any significant way. The other fundamental difference is that child language is entirely a *spoken language*, a much freer creature than written language. A recent introduction to child language isolated three skills which "distinguish the language of adults from the early language of the human child"—"a freedom from the here-and-now, the ability to take account of variations in shared knowledge, and an awareness of language forms." That a child makes little "reference to the past," and "none to the future" or "hypothetical events," that he is unaware that others do not share access to his own thoughts and past history, that he cannot "free the idea of a word from its referent," are crucial features germane to any discussion of the child in literature.[6]

At its extreme, child language shows several distinctive syntactic features. Even the earliest, pre-verbal features of child language, such as babbling, lallation (pronouncing *l* instead of *r*), and echolalia, which at first seem irrelevant to literary art, provide concepts for approaching the techniques and significance of sound poetry, where sound patterns almost entirely supplant semantics.[7] The one-word stage (maximum sentence length is one word) and the two-word stage are universal in the process of language acquisition. A survey article by Breyne Arlene Moskowitz in *Scientific American* summarizes current understanding of these early stages. At the one-word stage a child may use a "vertical construction (a series of one-word sentences) to express what an adult might say with a horizontal construction (a multiword sentence)."[8] Thus a child's sequence of "Car. Car. Go. Go. Bus. Bus. Bus." might express the idea that " 'Hearing that car reminds me that we went on the bus yesterday.' "[9] A simple poem in a sense, the 'car. go. bus.' sequence demonstrates the different syntactic patterning—synchronic, metonymic—which shapes the most primitive speech.

The two-word stage introduces a new element in language acquisition. It is a "time for experimenting with many binary semantic-syntactic relations such as possessor-possessed ('Mommy sock'), actor-action ('Cat sleeping') and action-object ('Drink soup')."[10] The vertical construction continues at this stage. The next stage of language acquisition (there is no three-word stage) is known as telegraphic speech: "characterized by short, simple sentences made up primarily of content words: words that are rich in semantic content, usually nouns and verbs. The speech is called telegraphic because the sentences lack function 'words': tense endings on verbs and plural endings on nouns, prepositions, conjunctions, articles and so on."[11] These stages are found, of course, in very young children: telegraphic speech is typical at thirty months. The older a child becomes, the less her language differs from the adult. And the youngest children are seldom the subject of fiction or poetry. Nonetheless, careful examination of the extremes defines the criteria by which we might separate one from the other. In other words, aside from the direct imitation of such features of child speech as two-word sentences, any writer is faced with a model of speech development from vertical to horizontal construction, from absorption in the here-and-now to the articulation of hypothetical events, from concrete nouns and verbs to abstractions and function words. Most writers interested in the distinctiveness of the child's point of view will, no matter what the age of the child they are dealing with, incline toward the beginning of these continuums.

These syntactic features overlap with the vocabulary and semantics of child language. Empirical studies confirm, for example, that a child's "early words are primarily concrete nouns and verbs; more abstract words such as adjectives are acquired later," and that naming is the first use for a newly acquired word.[12] More specifically, we know that the child's first fifty words typically name important persons, favourite foods, highlights of the daily routine, and common animals and their noises; also included are words used to effect a change in environment or to regulate interaction with parents (e.g., "ta," "more," "no," "up," "out").[13]

Similarly, other scholars have categorized the child's first sentences, identifying actions, possession, location, recurrence, nomination, and non-existence as the main meanings.[14] A more particular semantic feature, with more potential for illuminating a writer's language, is that "children first learn and apply words for objects at an intermediate level of generality ['flower' before 'tulip' or 'plant'], and only later learn their more specific names or the general categories into which they fall."[15]

Much of the entire process by which children learn the meanings of words is a beautiful mystery. But what *has* been described has its own special beauty for the student of literature, and for a sense of literary child languages. Moskowitz, for example, summarizes research by Eve V. Clark which shows that a child first uses a word to designate a specific object, but almost immediately generalizes the word to refer to many other objects. Later, as a child progresses, "the meanings of the words [are] narrowed down until eventually they more or less [coincide] with the meanings accepted by adult speakers of the language."[16] Here are two of a dozen sections of the chart Moskowitz includes as illustration:[17]

Child's lexical item	First referents	Other referents in order of occurrence	General area of semantic expansion
MOOI	MOON	Cake Round marks on windows Writing on windows and in books Round shapes in books Tooling on leather book covers Round postmarks Letter "O"	SHAPE

		Specks of dirt	
		Dust	
FLY	FLY	All small insects	SIZE
		Child's own toes	
		Crumbs of bread	
		A toad	

In this schematic reduction of a familiar process we may see convincing confirmation of the popular equation of child and poet. Seeing a cake, or the letter "O," as the moon, is exactly the sort of transformation that makes poetry possible, although the child would not be aware of the "O-ooo" of surprise, or the lovers' moon, which might give resonance to the poet's invention.

> Some overextensions might . . . represent the earliest signs of metaphoric usage in children's speech. As a criterion for saying that a child intends a word to be taken metaphorically, we usually require that the child have an option between using the literal or the metaphorical description of the object. . . . In his overextensions the child is overlooking a large number of dissimilarities between the objects and drawing attention to their similarity along some other dimension. This is a crucial aspect of our use of metaphor. The power of a metaphor seems to lie in the unexpectedness of the dimension of similarity and the way in which it captures the essence of the object being described in metaphorical terms.[18]

I would only add that the child in discovering a similarity between objects in one quite restricted dimension overlooks a large number of *similarities* as well. The hypothesis of a child's metaphor which is necessarily restricted to one narrow band of similarity surfaces frequently in this book.

Although critics have seldom considered the relationship between child language and the languages through which a writer represents the child, the subject of overgeneralization reminds us that from a broader perspective the science of linguistics has had a massive impact on literary criticism in the last twenty-five years.[19] As I have already implied, one of the central concepts of recent structuralist poetics is "firmly grounded in study of language acquisition among children."[20] Roman Jakobson's crucial distinction between two poles of linguistic performance, similarity and contiguity, led to the recognition of the basic dichotomy between metaphoric and metonymic processes in language. Robert Scholes summarizes the basic difference: "metaphorical substitution is based on a likeness or *analogy* between the literal word and its metaphorical replacement, while metonymical substitution is based on an *association* between the literal word and its substitute.''[21] Piaget has taught us that a child's reasoning is based on contiguity, and the possibilities of verbal, synchronic constructions for child languages affect several writers discussed in this book. But in the crucial area of semantics there is an exception.[22] While the child may not be capable of metaphor, in the sense of having "an option between . . . the literal or the metaphorical description,'' her semantics are definitely developed through a metaphorical process.

Child language clearly has a distinctive vocabulary and unique syntactic and semantic features. Early pronunciation is also distinctive: the reduction of consonant clusters at the beginning of words to a single consonant, the assimilation of all the consonants or vowels in a word to the same place of articulation in the mouth, and the preference for voiced initial consonants and unvoiced final consonants. Again, as throughout this quick review of the subject, I recognize the possibilities for using such objective observations to describe certain aspects of literary texts which readers have found successful in identifying and interpreting the child's point of view. But I have begun by giving a very truncated description of promising aspects of child language, before blurring the matter with literary considerations and empirical qualifications.

Roethke's thoughts on child language in "The Flight" describe a particular instance of an artistic problem; the general indication of the difficulty is simply that so few writers have attempted a sustained presentation of the pre-adolescent child's point of view. *Oliver Twist,* for example, which might be thought of as an early exception, has Oliver grown to age nine by the second chapter, and Dickens is so completely devoted to creating a vehicle for social commentary that we very rarely know how Oliver sees or feels or thinks.[23] Henry James demonstrates the difficulty by creating children so extraordinarily precocious that Muriel Shine, in *The Fictional Children of Henry James*, must conclude that "in the final analysis, his children are, without exception, deeply sentient miniature adults.''[24] James Joyce in *A Portrait of the Artist as a Young Man* and Thomas Wolfe in *Look Homeward, Angel* skip over the pre-adolescent years in a few pages. A novel such as W.O. Mitchell's *Who Has Seen the Wind,* discussed in Chapter 4, which is written for adults and entirely devoted to the pre-adolescent's view of the world, is an intriguing rarity.

Yet Mitchell's sense of child language is so fine that, not surprisingly, *Who Has Seen the Wind* has often been thought of as a novel speaking to children. On the other hand, writers for children may be more successful more often in convincingly articulating the child's point of view. The reckless neologisms of Dr. Seuss, the necessity to define in E.B. White's

Charlotte's Web, and the vocabulary of food and daily routine in Dennis Lee's nursery rhymes seem to echo child language more closely than in writers for adults. To many of these writers child language, of course, may offer little in the way of technique, may, indeed, only pose the danger of a "suite in goo-goo."

In speaking of autobiography—rather than the novel or poem—Richard Coe seems unequivocal on the danger of "overmuch realism in language":

> The language of childhood revisited is that of the adult. Perhaps by instinct, perhaps warned by the Awful Fate of Lewis Carroll's *Sylvie and Bruno*, scarcely one among our poets has fallen into the trap of carrying the search for literal truth to the point of reproducing the lisping (or whining) tones of the genuine child. In fact, among the greater writers, the opposite would seem to be true: the younger the child, the more adult the language.[25]

In adopting the term "child languages" I hope to have recognized both the common sense of this remark and the irony of the situation. One of the most intriguing aspects of Coe's excellent study is his later meditation on this paradox. "More than any other factor in human experience," he admits,

> it is the use of rational language which destroys the child's "intuitive" relationship with the world. Language creates distance between the self and the object; language generalizes, transforming a unique perception into a common one; language transmutes realities into abstractions, replacing the "being-there" . . . of the phenomenon by its measurable properties. On the other hand, the writer has no tool other than language at his disposal—hence the tendency . . . to use language to a greater or lesser degree *irrationally*, to prefer where possible poetry to prose, to break down overlogical linguistic structures into impressionistic, at times frankly incomprehensible, word-groupings . . . which rely on overtones, free associations, and images rather than on the formal patterns of grammar.[26]

It seems peculiarly essential to writing through this paradox that "the state of being 'without language' means in fact the state of having a language *different* from that of the adult, more individualized, less rational in structure, each word more immediately and directly related to specific phenomena than will be the case later on."[27] Some understanding of that different language, some sense of the way a child's understanding of the world is suggested by features of her language, will provide both description and appreciation of the writer's languages for childhood. Two brief examples may introduce the approach which this book tests.

One of the most familiar creations of the "as if" of a child's world in modern literature is James Joyce's *A Portrait of the Artist as a Young Man* (1916). His principal solution to the technical difficulty of maintaining "all interior drama" was, of course, a version of stream-of-consciousness:

> He could not get out the answer for the sum but it did not matter. White roses and red roses: those were beautiful colours to think of. And the cards for first place and second place and third place were beautiful colours too: pink and cream and lavender. Lavender and cream and pink roses were beautiful to think of. Perhaps a wild rose might be like those colours and he remembered the song about the wild rose blossoms on the little green place. But you could not have a green rose. But perhaps somewhere in the world you could.[28]

The flow of associated colours and images has neither the fragmented syntax nor the abrupt transitions we might expect of a boy's stream-of-consciousness. Although Joyce's language in the early part of the novel is rightly acclaimed for its richness of sensory detail, the effect is more of a sequence of ideas than of a clutter of sensations. The syntactically complete sentences put the emphasis on Stephen's thinking: "beautiful colours" do not register simply as visual sensations—they are things to be *thought of*. Stephen, even as child, Joyce implies, is more reflective thinker than actor.

The characterization is entirely apt, but how then is the early part of Joyce's novel thought to be so effective in expressing the interior drama of a child? The answer appears to lie in the later description of Stephen's first writing. When he thinks "himself into confidence," "all these elements which he deemed common and insignificant fell out of the scene."[29] Stephen discovers that learning to write means learning to discriminate and choose and exclude. After the novel's first chapter, the stream-of-consciousness is replaced by a more conventional indirect narration reflecting the ordering and selection in Stephen's older mind. This startling shift, despite Joyce's emphasis on thinking, by contrast highlights the stream-of-consciousness, a *different* language closer to the syntax of the young child. The early part of the novel conveys energetically, with concrete nouns and verbs and a corresponding absence of subordinate clauses and passives, the equivalence of varied sensations *and* ideas in the child's mind. The colours of the roses, and the cards for first, second and third place, the remembered song, and the imagined roses are each of equal value. The young Stephen's mind does not work toward a conclusion. Both "you could not have a green rose" and "perhaps somewhere you could" have equal weight. So, similarly, on the novel's opening page (where, for but a few moments, Joyce directly invokes child language), the story, his father's appearance, the song, the wet bed, and the smell of his mother are equally momentous in the young mind. *A Portrait's* particular limited stream-of-consciousness intensifies the egotistic self-absorption of the child mind.

Appreciation of Joyce's portrait of young Stephen begins, as I have said, in the impression of layer upon layer of exquisitely discrete sensations.[30] The reason that an overload of images should be so often a technique associated with the child is obvious. If childhood is conceived, simplistically, as pre-literate and pre-sexual, then the child apprehends his world wholly through the senses. The Romantic preference for a "life of sensations" reinforces the bias. Peter Coveney describes the limits of this technique for expressing the child's view (contrasted, incidentally, to the "psychological realities of Joyce's portrait") in Virginia Woolf's *The Waves*:

> The early episodes deal with the sensations of the children in their garden near the sea, and then when they go to school. There is no attempt at rendering their sensations into a child-language; the diction is in fact heavily stylized. Everything lies in the sensuous responses of the children to their environment. But there is not enough differentiation made (at least, if it is there, it is not easily to be perceived) between the characters; there is only the highest common factor of their sensitivity. There is little sense of their development.[31]

In Canadian literature the best example of this tendency is Ernest Buckler's *The Mountain and the Valley*. But Buckler's heavily stylized prose, as my discussion in Chapter 5 shows, is as far from the temptation to "overmuch realism" as any writer we might contemplate. The possibilities for literary child languages go well beyond the dream of the totally sensory. They go ultimately to the "at times frankly incomprehensible" limit of a poet like bill bissett. But again at this extreme, with a poet who very rarely writes about children, some understanding of child language allows us to refine the description and to appreciate a central aspect of bissett's eccentric work. In Chapter 9 I discuss the poet's phonetic spelling, his use of repetition for learning and transforming, his diction and the prominent conjunction "and." One feature, which we may see in the poem "yu sing," will serve as an illustration. Whereas the fashion in contemporary lyrics is to drop articles, bissett's style is remarkable for his insistent, obsessive use of the definite article. Like a child, he overuses the definite article for the first mention of an object: "th dragon,/dreaming, is/inside th tea."[32] The linguist would say the speaker is egocentrically assuming shared knowledge when it does not exist. For bissett, presumably, this implication of child language is part of his meaning: he wants to transcend barriers, to insist that on some magic, uncomprehended level the reader shares "privileged access . . . to his thoughts and past experience."[33] The child doesn't deceive; he has a faith that his listener will make every effort to understand.

Perhaps bissett uses his own form of child language to escape the "patterns" which language "place[s] upon their [children's] understandings."[34] He aspires to the condition where language has an initiatory function, but has not yet acquired an inhibiting one. This dream makes bissett an extremely interesting writer for students of child language. But it also makes him peripheral, because as Coe points out, in learning a language the child is learning a rational pattern for organizing the world and its properties, its morality and esthetics. The development of pattern is the source of our absorption, both lay and professional, in the way children talk. And the impossibility of remembering our own childish talk, like our appreciation of the writer's difficulty in translating the talk, only intensifies the fascination.

The proliferating studies of psycholinguists, valuable as they are, do nothing to diminish this fascination. Ruth Weir's *Language in the Crib* (1962) continues to be compelling reading, despite the existence of more subtle techniques than she applied (such as highly sophisticated electronic pitch analysis), because it records so faithfully long strings of pre-sleep monologue. But the multiplication of psycholinguistic studies of child language does create complications. The single universal child language that I posited to earlier in this chapter only becomes more difficult to define. Obviously a child's language is different at different ages. The recent trend to studies of pragmatics reveals how sharply the form and function of a single child's language will vary according to the specific situation in which it is used. As Iona and Peter Opie showed in *The Lore and Language of Schoolchildren* (1959), the language of playground and classroom is so different that the child might be said to be naturally bilingual. In short, as I have implied, my term "child languages" might also be more suitable for students of language acquisition.[35]

If so, then a certain randomness in this book may be justified. I have organized the study as a series of closely related essays, rather than as a single sustained argument, because the essence of my "argument" is that there is no end to child languages. I believe that a reading (far from complete) of empirical studies of child language has helped me to recognize aspects of language I might otherwise have ignored, has helped me to see distinguishing features in the writer's articulation of a child's mind. But I have not attempted to name every book that includes children, nor even every book that imagines the child's mind with effective uniqueness. I have, rather, watched for those contact points between Canadian literature and studies of child language acquisition which seemed to me to set off the most sparks. In doing so, I hope I have also respected the individual talents of several very different writers in different genres.

Obviously my approach does not result in a definitive taxonomy of strategies for writing about children. I have, however, tried to order the various essays, testing various hypotheses, as a movement which might be conveniently labelled from conventional to unconventional, or in Coe's terms, from the writers using a rational grammar to those testing the limits of irrationality. The book moves from the universal topic of the child-self as subject remembered in Margaret Laurence and Alice Munro, to the eccentrically unusual fusion of writer with his own child language realized in the poetry of bill bissett. Following this line takes me from discussion of the sociology of the bewildered child in the short fiction of Clark Blaise, to W. O. Mitchell's sensitive study of language development in *Who Has Seen the Wind*, to the paradoxically ornate naïveté of Ernest Buckler, and to what seems to me the closest approach to writing in the language of a child in Emily Carr. At this limit, I have turned to reflect on child languages in other genres—in the long tradition of the lyric poem, and in the exceptional spontaneity of James Reaney's plays. The poets' and playwrights' resistance to the overlogical in language seemed to lead naturally to the contemporary nursery-rhymer, Dennis Lee, and then to bissett.

Growing up, as Tom Robbins agonizes, too often means stopping growing, too often implies the social pressure to stop the process "of change and renewal" which is inevitable in youth.[36] As much as a sense of stages and a single image of child language is helpful to my inquiry, I must insist that child language is magical partly because it is a process so rapid and so beyond complete description that we can only marvel. As the intersections between child language and imagined child languages multiply I hope our understanding of child language(s) will continue to grow, but never "grow up."

2

The Language of Childhood Remembered: Alice Munro and Margaret Laurence

In those days I was a young girl, but didn't know it. . . .

Alice Munro, "Tell Me Yes or No"

This was my territory in the time of my youth, and in a sense my life since then has been an attempt to look at it, to come to terms with it. Stultifying to the mind it certainly could be, and sometimes was, but not to the imagination.

Margaret Laurence, "Where the World Began"

Coming to terms with one's youth might be said to be the subject of all literature. As Chapter 1 indicates, in this book I am mainly interested in a particular aspect of the process: where coming to terms involves the convincing representation of a pre-adolescent child's perspective. The strategies available to a writer for this purpose are as varied as the dialect speech in *Huckleberry Finn* and the stream-of-baby-tuckoo-consciousness which opens *A Portrait of the Artist as a Young Man.* An adult writer's child languages range from those attempting an unmediated replication of a sandbox incantation to those making an inquiring assessment of the significance of a child's limited perspective. On this continuum Margaret Laurence's *A Bird in the House* (1970) and Alice Munro's *Lives of Girls and Women* (1971) come close to the limit of inquiry. Much of these two books is concerned with adolescence, but both writers show a great deal of interest in the younger child's perception, particularly in how it will, remembered and reassessed, reveal or shape the adult narrator's self.

The particulars of this approach, the forms, grammar, and style by which an adult narrator relates to her perception as a child, describe the language of childhood remembered. Here are two instances of child language as specific subject, the first from Laurence, the second from Munro:

> My grandmother was a Mitigated Baptist. I knew this because I had heard my father say, "At least she's not an unmitigated Baptist," and when I enquired, he told me that if you were Unmitigated you believed in Total Immersion, which meant that when you were baptised you had to be dunked in the Wachakwa River with all your clothes on.[1]

> I loved the sound of that word [tomb] when I first heard her [Aunt Elspeth] say it. I did not know exactly what it was, or had got it mixed up with womb, and I saw us inside some sort of hollow marble egg, filled with blue light, that did not need to get in from outside.[2]

Both narrators are writers, interested in the potential of language: here each uses an instance of a child's incomplete understanding of the standard vocabulary and semantics to make a particular point. Yet the passages are sharply different. Vanessa/Laurence uses the child's formation (generalizing the rule that the negative of a negative equals the positive root word) as part of her narration in the fictional present (however indeterminate that might be). She explains the origin of the term "mitigated," but only insofar as it is possible to do so and maintain the child's point of view. To the end of her explanation she respects the validity of a child's formation of concepts, most obviously by turning a general adjective into the label for a unique religious denomination. She continues to be incorrect, from an adult perspective, on semantics. The cumbersome predication ("which meant that when"), the colloquial use of the second person, the absence of any vocabulary implying judgement, and the verb "dunked" (which reduces the ritual to tea-and-cookies mannerism) all reinforce the sense of a child speaking. Thus, Laurence not only achieves humour through refraining from comment, but she also implicitly acknowledges the integrity of a child language different from that of the adult: from its perspective her grandmother is as gentle and forgiving in her religion as in her personal relationships.

Rather than using the child's word to extend her own adult vocabulary, Del/Munro reports on her memory of her reaction as a child. The child's understanding of language is described by the adult, not used by the writer. Laurence recognizes the source of her misapprehension; Munro is uncertain of hers. This single comparison shows Del to be more writerly, in two ways. First, she reacts consciously to the aural, sub-semantic aspect of the word.

And, second, she moves from her memory of her first reaction to the word, not to use the child language, but to explain the concept resting in the child's mind through an intensely imagistic analogy—egg, marble, and blue light mingled. To be sure we might sense a hint of the child's language in the literalist logic of the circumlocution, "that did not need to get in from outside," but the essence of Munro's strategy is to give authenticity to the child's perspective, not by using the child's language, or by recreating a child's logic, or lack of logic, but by exploiting the most sophisticated sensory analogies, to evoke the magically elusive and incomplete dream world of the child. In this respect Munro seems closer to Ernest Buckler than to Emily Carr.

Clearly Laurence and Munro present their childhood perceptions in sharply different modalities. Yet often the reader of these two novels will think she is reading two variations, or interpretations, of the same novel. Both works, published a year or so apart, contain eight stories, told in the first person, which combine to form a novel of hesitant, sometimes awkward, growing up. In both books middle-aged narrators, apparently writers, remember their childhood and adolescence and their separateness as youthful writers-dreamers. Heredity is a central subject for both Laurence and Munro: what links the lives of girls, adolescents, and women? What is the "intricate structure of lives supporting [them] from the past" (*LGW*, 26)? Both Del Jordan and Vanessa MacLeod have to come to terms with the "steel-spined" (*BH*, 34) and the "theatrical" (*LGW*, 83) in their community's puritanical religion. An organizing motif in one novel, such as war in *A Bird in the House* or photographs in *Lives of Girls and Women*, echoes in a minor key in the other work. The novels even seem to share specific moments: the child narrator's parenthetic digression into logic in the midst of rampant fantasy, or her first view of a corpse. And both novels, I have already suggested, evolve a form from a double vision: the child's experience, and the adult narrator's use of that experience and language. The adult narrator learns in some way from the imagining, the creating, the remembering, the retelling of the child's perspective. My very uncertainty about the right word to describe this process may imply my focus. What are the features—of macrotext and microtext, of genre and of syntax—which differentiate the child language in two novels with such remarkable and fundamental similarities?

In *A Bird in the House* Laurence tells us the stories of Vanessa MacLeod's growing up. The dominant voice is the one we hear at the end of the last story, the Vanessa of about age forty remembering her youth in Manawaka, discovering the connection between remembered experience and present self. In other words, Laurence does not attempt a technique like Emily Carr's, which moves the reader totally into the 'here-and-now' of the child's world, where the teller assumes no difference between the child's and the reader's knowledge. But within the remembering consciousness the child's perspective is often incorporated for its own sake: the explanation of the use of "Mitigated" is the one the child would give, if asked. Thus, as Vanessa continually reassesses her childhood experiences and opinions, she also cherishes the integrity of those experiences and opinions. Munro's Del Jordan, on the other hand, always makes us aware of the limitations of these experiences and opinions.

The Depression, for example, is barely a ripple under the surface of Laurence's stories, not a desperate concern, but a comment overheard at the edge of Vanessa's consciousness: " 'They've all got stenographers already, for pity's sake, or else they can't afford to hire one. Won't this damn Depression ever be over?' " (*BH*, ll). The child's sense of the economy of the time is right not only for Manawaka's relative good fortune, but for the family's reluctance to talk about money and for her grandmother's eternal dream of being a lady.

When Aunt Edna tells Vanessa that she had lost five boyfriends to her grandfather's strict dislike of smoking, the memory is summed up in this way: "At the time I imagined, because she was laughing, that she thought it was funny" (*BH*, 15). The phrase "at the time" indicates that the adult Vanessa, the narrator, has now reconsidered her youthful opinion. But Laurence makes her effect—so characteristic of her child language—not by giving her adult judgement but by reporting her child view, and its origin.

In "Horses of the Night" Laurence makes an explicit reference to the process which seems to govern the mind-style of the novel. Reunited with her now older cousin Chris, at his own home, Vanessa realizes that he has not mentioned the two horses, Duchess and Firefly, that galloped magically through his stories of "up north": "I guess I had known for some years now, without realising it, that the pair had only ever existed in some other dimension" (*BH*, 124). Significantly, although the pattern of development in the novel, however slight, is found in gradual realizations of what Vanessa has "known for some years," the possibility of *knowing* without *realizing* is respected throughout the book, as it is, to be sure, in *The Stone Angel*, and especially in *The Diviners*, where knowledge beyond language is so central a concern. Furthermore, this passage, in its tentative "I guess," does not dismiss the "other dimension" but remembers its importance: "stultifying to the mind it certainly could be," remarks Laurence recalling her youth, "but not to the imagination."

This tension between imagining child and narrating adult has not struck all readers as particularly productive. Leona Gom feels that "memories become memoirs," and wonders "whether the sacrifice of the more immediate perceptions of the experiencing Vanessa is worth the restrained style of the adult. The distance between the two characters is too great for the reader to accept Vanessa's credibility as a child, or to participate in the life which she herself looks back on with relative uninvolvement."[3] Helen Hoy finds an "implausible and irritating disingenuousness" precisely at those points where the narrator remembers her childhood naïveté with such "complacency, delight, indulgence."[4] Ronald Labonté, on the other hand, seems closer to my own point of view, when, noting that Laurence always puts character before technique, he claims that she "give[s] us . . . a drama of perceiving and being perceived," and suggests that the narrating voice "gives us room and time to flex our own memory bank muscles, to make associations with the characters' emotional reactions instead of with their predicaments."[5] Undoubtedly, Laurence is not a writer of great technical virtuosity, but her use of the storyteller, her exploring the implications of songs and mottoes learned while very young, and of a child's understanding of metaphor, contribute to a significant category of child language in *A Bird in the House.*

I suspect some of the discontent with the novel may arise in the child Vanessa's principal role as "professional listener" (*BH*, 8). Leslie Fiedler acidly expressed reaction to this figure of "Child as Peeping Tom," which he finds originating in Henry James. "Such children," he goes on, "are the presiding geniuses of modern fiction" and evidence of "the last genteel reticence; a refusal to portray the child as an actual sinner though it is no longer possible to postulate his innocence as absolute."[6] Although Vanessa herself becomes more aware of the feelings of those who are listened to, and even "sickened" (*BH*, 64) by her own eavesdropping, readers might still find it difficult to avoid a reaction like Fiedler's.

Here, as elsewhere, the child's *reaction* to what she hears—for example, the furious vision of a gallery of dolls which follows Aunt Edna's allusion to the Depression (*BH*, 11)—has its own, not fully comprehended, or at least articulated, appropriateness. So, the occasional use of child language, either as the directly quoted " 'Gee' " (*BH*, 7) or " 'keen' " (*BH*, 119), or as a part of the narrator's account ("I watched the man whoa the team . . . " [*BH*, 133]), suggests that complete identification of the two Vanessas is unnecessary. The young Vanessa is different. In writing this way Laurence is insisting that the older Vanessa, whatever her adult knowing, senses that the child may see and express things in ways that are not available to the adult: the older Vanessa is, in a way, listening to another dialect, sometimes seeing through it things she had not thought possible, sometimes, of course, no longer comprehending.[7]

Memory is not the same as knowing. The novel moves not so much to knowledge, that is to that "lightning burst of knowingness" (*BH*, 117) that Vanessa dreams of when she is with Chris, but to a recognition of limitations. We find Vanessa at the end of the novel climbing back into the loft in the stable, "as I had done when I was a child" (*BH*, 177). The loft is a place less conducive to momentous revelation than simply to "remember[ing] myself remembering" (*BH*, 178). In that process, the narrator often senses the merit of a child's perception and the limitation in its loss.

This appreciation seems to be involved, for example, in Vanessa's late discovery of her father's secret love, intuited, almost unexpressed, and almost avoided by Vanessa the narrator. The child's failure to catch her father's hints about the positive side of his going to war (*BH*, 79) is given integrity by the narrator's hesitant remembering: she has a sense of the validity of the unknown and unspoken, a respect for limits. The curious relationship between words and the unworded has a good deal to do with the child language in *A Bird in the House*. Among Vanessa's dozen "secret sanctuaries" (*BH*, 1), which themselves suggest Freudian implications of re-entry into childhood, the most important are the scribblers where she does her writing: words, to be sure, have a magic fascination. Yet, Vanessa's interest derives less from a writer's knowledge of possible meanings than from a learning child's emphasis on meaning inherent in the surrounding situation: "I was hardly aware of her meaning. I was going instead by the feel of the words" (*BH*, 30). This sense in which a restricted code touches Laurence's prose will emerge more clearly by extending the comparison with Alice Munro.

In *Lives of Girls and Women* the young Del is also interested in words and language. But her interest is clearly in a different narrative framework. The perspective is, perhaps, most clearly marked near the end of the sequence, when in "Baptizing" Del waits for Garnet French and yet does not want him to come. Munro marks this ambivalence with the time-honoured symbol of the mirror: "I was amazed to think that the person suffering was me, for it was not me at all; I was watching. I was watching, I was suffering" (*LGW*, 200). Such watching of self describes her narrative angle throughout: while Laurence/Vanessa typically watches others, Del watches her other self. For her, child language, and her perspective as a child are *watched*—as her identification with the photographer in the "Epilogue" insists—"with absolute sincerity, absolute irony" (*LGW*, 200), from adulthood.

In "Heirs of the Living Body," for example, Del gives her reaction to her mother's story about cousin Mary Agnes: " 'She was deprived of oxygen in the birth canal. Uncle Bob Oliphant held Aunt Moira's legs together on the way to the hospital because the doctor had told them she might hemorrhage' " (*LGW*, 33). Characteristically, Del's point of view as child is in the form of a question: "Would he have his pipe in his mouth while he held Aunt Moira's legs, would he give businesslike assent to her commotion, just as he did to Boston Blackie's?" (*LGW*, 34). Instead of the narrator's declarative "I imagined" or, even, "I wondered if," which would keep the young Del's speculation more or less sealed within the child's moral framework, Munro's use of a rhetorical question (implying an undoubted "yes" answer), and her shift to the present tense, make her relatives' ludicrousness part of Del's attitude in the fictional present. In short, the narrator shows a good deal of the same "nimble malice" that she detects in her aunts' hypocritical "courtesies" (*LGW*, 33).

As my opening quotations showed, Munro studiously explains the child's confusions of standard language. Del always seems so diligently intellectual, particularly when we compare *Lives*, for example, with Emily Carr's language of Small, discussed in Chapter 6. At the beginning of the book Del, remembering a particular instance of her child language, explains how she imagined quicksand, itself probably something imagined by Uncle Benny, "shining, with a dry-liquid roll—I had it mixed up with quicksilver" (*LGW*, 2). The child's process of language learning apparently has no merit either for its novel understanding of sand or mercury or for its revelation of the young Del. An adult sense of a distinguishable past and present is integral to the grammar of the story. In the frequent references to Del's childhood understanding, the qualifiers always reminds us of the inadequacy of the child's knowing: "Later on she was to find she did not belong in Jubilee either, but *at present* she took hold of it hopefully . . ."; "*As yet* I followed her without embarrassment, *enjoying* the commotion" (*LGW*, 6, 7; my italics). Just as Munro shows such exquisite skill with the fine moral or emotional distinction, so she is perhaps most convincing when she describes the child's feelings in passages whose accumulation of modifiers and startling analogies mark a distance from the language of a child. Del, for instance, remembers her mother in church: "She would sit looking all around, cautious but unabashed, like an anthropologist taking note of the behaviour of a primitive tribe. She listened to the sermon bolt upright, bright-eyed, skeptically chewing at her lipstick; I was afraid that at any moment she might jump up and challenge something" (*LGW*, 80). The reader is, I think, increasingly aware, although we do not even know as much about Del the writer/narrator as about the adult Vanessa, that Munro/Del's style expresses so many of the attitudes—"taking note," "skeptically," "challenging[ly]" (*LGW*, 80)—that she attributes to her own mother's reaction to what she hears.

"Up there," Munro might have written in the opening story, "we were in a house as small and shut up as any boat is on the sea . . . ." To interpolate into this passage, where I have broken it after the opening phrase, the comment: "you discovered what you never remembered down in the kitchen" (*LGW*, 22), shifts the emphasis sharply away from the child's vision as experienced, toward the child's reaction reconstructed and assessed. In concluding "The Flats Road," Del comments of the mysterious Madeleine: "We remembered her like a story" (*LGW*, 23). The simile echoes continuously throughout the book, for Del's recall, it seems, is triggered not by the "sensation" given us by "some material object," as in Proust, nor by some pattern of associations, but by story.[8] The narrator recalls what has been given the shape of narrative in childhood. *Lives of Girls and Women* has the form of a mélange of stories, overheard, recalled, told, retold; it is a story about the stories an adult remembers from childhood, and adolescence; the title seems to direct us to this multiplicity. Thus, unlike many of the texts I will discuss in this book, there is little nostalgia for, and not much regret about childhood in Munro. She listens to the stories of childhood, as a storyteller herself, slightly cynically for what she might learn. When she recounts Aunt Elspeth's explanation of Uncle Craig's not running for election, the literary allusion to Melville's Bartleby—" 'He preferred not' " (*LGW*, 32)—warns us that accurate remembering, or the child's response, are minor concerns.

From Uncle Benny's story of mysterious holes in the Wawanash River to her dreamed novel of the Sherriffs, Del's childhood is made up of stories, or of the promise of story, "not real but true" (*LGW*, 206). In such a childhood, the language of the child is a curiosity, a storytelling strategy, a part of a bizarre narrative, not a phenomenon to be imitated for its own authentic vision of the world. Del's occasional, but quite noticeable, recall of specific instances of child language serves, as we have seen, to establish perspective, to make an ironic or satiric point. Her constant and aggressive remembering of child story provides her sense of connections: life conceived in terms of, for example, strong character, identifiable motive, suspense, adventure, and evocative setting, but not, perhaps, of clear endings.

As an encyclopedia reader, "famous for my memory" (*LGW*, 136), Del is tempted by lists, but they are clearly inadequate and unsatisfactory. As much as they embarrass her, her mother's stories are a more congenial narrative device: biting in her assessment of the characters, transparently exaggerated, and filled with hints of unstated evil, and victimization. Munro's *Lives* include the stories of Del's mother's childhood, and even pieces of her grandmother's stories. The story "Princess Ida" is an illustration of the method of the novel as accumulating child stories. Del quotes portions of her mother's story about her religious fanatic mother: " 'Well. My mother took her money and she ordered a great box of Bibles' " (*LGW*, 64). But Del tells the story as she remembers it from her own story-constructing childhood: "Yes, and the bush near and spooky, with the curious unconnected winds that lift the branches one by one. She would go into the house and find the fire out, the stove cold, the grease from the men's dinner thickened on the plates and pans" (*LGW*, 63). That she later hears a completely different story of her grandmother from her Uncle Bill (*LGW*, 74-75) only emphasizes the method of the novel. Child language for Alice Munro is the language of a child telling a story, particularly of a child telling a story to herself, or imagining a story. The curious validity of these massed stories (including stories within stories) reflects in the structure of the complete work that taste for catalogues so evident in Del's sensibility. Margaret Laurence appears to speak Vanessa's story; Alice Munro in a much more writerly way assembles Del's multiple stories, combining the oral, the written and the purely imagined (dreamed) dimensions of story. The narrator seems constantly aware of how experience has been shaped into, and has been shaped by, narrative.

So prominent are multiple stories in Munro's novel that the narrator's affection for the details of the language appears frequently as the story inherent in a simple word: "Sometimes, just by using a word like *barbaric*, she could make a pool of silence, of consternation round her" (*LGW*, 47). Single words, such as "nonsense," "*fuck*," "*pleasure*" (*LGW*, 122, 139, 181), almost tell their own stories. Each sets off the story-making imagination, with a sense of character, a hint of narrative, a touch of suspense: "I liked the word *mistress*, a full-skirted word, with some ceremony about it; a mistress should not be too slim" (*LGW*, 153).

That Del's childhood and youth is presented as a collage of stories heard, read, remembered and imagined, points to the obvious appropriateness of the macro-structure of the novel, interlinked but discrete short stories. This general form also complements Laurence's account of Vanessa's growing up; when her subject is the character of adult and aging women she uses a more traditional novel structure. One feature that the serial novel makes possible, indeed almost demands, is the frequent repetition of narrative information (about setting or relationships) as if it were new information. The allusion to Uncle Dan, identified as Grandfather's brother and a horse-trader, in the third story, for example, startles the reader who already has this information from the lengthy appearance of Dan in the first story of the sequence. On the one hand, this recurrence is an inevitable result of collecting stories originally prepared for separate publication—a weakness or an oversight perhaps. Yet, as I have discussed at more length in Chapter 6, this technique can help to authenticate the child's point of view by suggesting a narrating consciousness which is unable to remove itself from the moment of the telling in order to take account of past and future.

When the stories are read in sequence as sections of a novel, the convention of chronology, which has been a central concern in much Laurence criticism, is less tyrannical. Vanessa is ten at the beginning of the first story, ten-and-a-half in the third, and twelve at the opening of "A Bird in the House," the pivotal section of the novel; she is, however, eleven as "The Loons" opens, and only six at the beginning of "Horses of the Night." Thus Grandmother Connor dies in the third story and calms Grandfather Connor in the sixth. We have, then, an ideal form for the reassessment of childhood, of the past, of memory—the unconscious reassessment—by the narrating consciousness. In "A Bird in the House" the death of Vanessa's father affects her concept of heaven, drives her to unthinking violence, and alters her life: "Everything changed after my father's death" (*BH*, 93). In "The Loons" the same death, whose actual occurrence is always avoided, is announced almost as an aside: "That winter my father died of pneumonia, after less than a week's illness" (*BH*, 103). In the single story this sentence might escape notice; in the novel it stands out because it marks, possibly, an alternate response on the part of the young girl. It certainly suggests an acceptance by the narrator, but it also shows two authentic responses of the child.

Thus, although the Vanessa MacLeod stories contain a quite accessible *histoire*—that is, we could readily construct a fairly detailed chronology of the key events in Vanessa's life, especially between the ages of ten and twenty—the *discours*, particularly her assembling of eight discrete stories, works to diminish the importance of chronology.[9] Both Laurence and Munro seem to be looking for an alternative to the *Bildungsroman* for fictionalizing their childhood. Perhaps they distrust the *Bildungsroman*, with its elements of the rebellious youth rejecting his provincial origins and setting out on his own to seek love, vocation, and fortune, as an implicitly male genre.[10] Anthony Dawson seems to hint at the alternative when he describes the movement of *A Bird in the House* and *Lives of Girls and Women* (which he sees describing coming of age in Canada) as "going from definiteness to indefiniteness, from conviction to hesitation, certainty to uncertainty."[11] The wave-like movement of the serial novel reinforces this impression.

In Laurence, for example, the submerged chronological sequence is far less crucial than the arrangement of the stories in order of increasing temporal perspective. The first story takes place within a few hours on a single afternoon; the last story moves from age twelve-and-a-half to Grandfather Connor's death, when Vanessa is twenty, and then to a narrative vantage point another twenty years later. This is the first time we are given a glimpse of the presentness of the ostensible narrating consciousness. Laurence, thus, turns our attention away from a girl's growing up and turning away and changing to an adult's continually fitting her younger selves into the time span of her life.

Vanessa's growing social awareness, her allegiance to misfits further and further from her own family (Uncle Dan, then Piquette, then Harvey Shinwell), her increasing exercise of judgement and intellectual independence: all these experiences are undoubtedly part of the novel's progression. But one story does not replace another, so that the final recognition of her heritage does not *eliminate* the uncertainty of fearing and fighting the old man, but *adds* the seeing of him in still another way. Significantly enough, the memory of her youngest self, awed by Grandfather Connor, makes this acceptance possible. "*A-hoo-gah! A-hoo-gah!* I was gazing with love and glory at my giant grandfather as he drove his valiant chariot through all the streets of this world" (*BH*, 154). The child's adolescent perspective and the adult's awareness co-exist as different or blended modulations of the same experience. When Vanessa reflects on her mother's attempt to comfort her after she has lost her first man, she notes, "after a while it did not hurt so much. And yet twenty years later it was still with me to some extent, part of the accumulation of happenings which can never entirely be thrown away" (*BH*, 174). This sense of a sensation, an experience, an emotion disappearing, and yet continuing to exist in some form is fundamental to the effect of the serial novel.

In *Lives of Girls and Women*, of course, the general form of a novel made from discrete short stories contains such disappearing and continuing in the tumbling stories Del remembers. In the disclaimer, on the copyright page, Munro describes the novel as "autobiographical in form," a categorization that readily suggests the *Bildungsroman*. Yet, again, as with Laurence, the feminist theme and the serial form point to the *Bildungsroman* as a convention to be subverted. That Del, as remembered, is always a part of Jubilee, and that the sequence ends with a story called "Baptizing," are indications that growing up for girls and women demands a form at least tangential to the conventional novel. Munro's series of stories about stories, shows us many different sides of the same lives. Del's way of seeing her life is closer to the way Mr. Chamberlain remembers the war than her father's: more a "conglomeration of stories, leading nowhere in particular," than "an overall design, marked off in campaigns, which had a purpose, which failed or succeeded" (*LGW*, 125).

But despite the conglomeration, certain sequences of development clearly shape the novel. The most obvious is the gradual sexual initiation, from whispered fantasies and insulting obscenities through nudity and intercourse to her one friend's unwanted pregnancy. The girl's search for a relationship with her mother is also an important narrative element. The novel should also be seen, I think, in three movements: the world of the "ordinary," the interlude of the operetta at the book's centre, and the world of "self-forgetfulness" and "possibilities" (*LGW*, 108-10). But whatever the sense of beginning, middle and end in *Lives of Girls and Women*, any examination of the *discours* of the novel reveals a much more turbulent carnival of competing stories. At the end of "Changes and Ceremonies" Munro shows us four images of Miss Farris, prime mover of the operetta which so transforms the school and Del: "Though there is no plausible way of hanging those pictures together—if the last one is true then must it not alter the others?—they are going to have to stay together now" (*LGW*, 118). Here Munro gives us a way to read the structure of the novel, to question how one story alters another, to see that the remembered stories of childhood, and the stories we make up of our childhood are going to have to stay together, ironically commenting on one another, and altering one another.

In *A Bird in the House* the device of memory through story is not overt. Indeed, the forms of discourse in Vanessa's childhood are not nearly so closely associated with story. But of both works we may ask what the forms that give verbal shape to the childhoods of two girls might reveal about their styles as adult storytellers. In *A Bird in the House*, three verbal forms are particularly prominent in shaping the young Vanessa. There are the dialogues which Vanessa as often overhears as hears. Songs, and hymns, as the title of the first story makes explicit, are a key to her remembering. Mottoes and biblical tags are a third significant verbal form and, by their nature, perhaps the most insistent. Each of these is reflected, even if unconsciously for the narrator, in the style of the work, and in its respect for the unverbalized.

The high proportion of direct speech and dialogue in Laurence's stories is convincing, and convincingly remembered, probably because of its almost Pinteresque banality. For the most part Laurence's characters talk in stock formulas, repetitive clichés, and dead metaphors. If this is credible on the one hand, it can be, in its lack of resonance, in its absence of all but a single level of meaning, rather tedious.

References to song are concentrated in two or three stories. Song, for both Uncle Dan and for Aunt Edna at the piano, is an expression, however ineffectual, of freedom and rebellion. Vanessa herself intuits this aspect of song when she yells out "*I'm a poor lonesome cowboy*" (*BH*, 77) to avoid facing the oppressive implications of the Remembrance Day ceremony. The singers often rebel against the rigid behaviour demanded by mottoes. Vanessa recites some of the Scots family mottoes in "To Set Our House in Order": "*Be then a wall of brass. Learn to suffer. Consider the end. Go carefully*" (*BH*, 38). Although she implies here that even as a child she had an ironic attitude to such ethics of self-denial, the reiteration of such mottoes throughout the book demonstrates that they are an inescapable part of the narrator's own being. It takes great effort, the reader feels, for her to acknowledge at the end of the book that she has counselled her own children with the same "clichés of affection" (*BH*, 178) she heard from her mother, mottoes many generations old.

These three verbal forms that shape Vanessa's memory of her childhood are most obviously related in their indefiniteness. The women's kitchen dialogue, the ballads and hymns, and the puritan mottoes, share a restricted vocabulary, taciturnity, and an inclination to the formulaic. All contain metaphors that have lost their metaphoric value. All tend to communicate less by the meanings of the words than by their "feel." Basil Bernstein's terms, "restricted code" and "elaborated code," differentiate a language-user restricted "to the meanings implicit in the immediate situation" and a speaker "more able to generalize, to symbolize, more distanced and ironic." Much of what Vanessa overhears is a restricted code, with "many pronouns and other pro-forms such as 'thing,' 'stuff,' 'do,' 'get,' etc." Clearly the term "restricted code" is unsuitable to describe Margaret Laurence's language in *A Bird in the House*. Nevertheless, I would argue that her appreciation of the values implicit in such a code (in Aunt Edna, in Piquette, in Chris's family, eventually perhaps, in her own childhood) is not only a subject of the novel, but is covertly reinforced by a certain simplicity of syntax and spareness of vocabulary. Laurence knows the limitation of the restricted code, but she also respects it as "an instrument of solidarity within [a] group, and a medium for intimacy between individuals."[12]

In other words, a primarily oral use of language in Vanessa's childhood becomes, despite the young girl's own reading and writing and dreaming, the key to her adult recounting of her childhood. Thus, although we witness Vanessa doing a great deal more writing than Del Jordan, the narration of her story appears to be spoken aloud. The ways in which Laurence's writing uses features of the spoken language appear to be what Ronald Labonté has in mind when he distinguishes the "lazy tenor of Laurence's voice" from "the harder-edged utterings of Alice Munro."[13] This strategy also affects Laurence's insistence, most pronounced in *The Diviners*, on the importance of the unworded, on the knowledge of the unlettered. Since child language is entirely spoken, and is learned almost entirely from spoken language, the characteristics of speech in *A Bird in the House* themselves give support to the value of the child's view and expression.

Vanessa, we know, "loved to talk about" herself (*BH*, 18). Presumably one of the attributes she shares with her grandfather, however reluctant she is to admit it, is that when "he could think of nothing else to do, he would sit me down on a footstool beside his chair and make me listen, fidgeting with boredom, while he talked of the past" (*BH*, 6). So, although there is no identified audience within the fiction, Laurence often writes as if there is a listener to a tale being spoken. "That house in Manawaka," she begins, "is the one which, more than any other, I carry with me" (*BH*, 1). By the use of the demonstrative "that," she assumes an audience already familiar with the house; she presents herself as suddenly being recorded in the midst of her telling someone of her childhood. Even the more writerly parts of the narration are likely to seem somewhat of an interpolation designed to give a mythic (and, therefore, more readily memorable) dimension to her personal story. Again, on the opening page, we read "On the lawn a few wild blue violets dared to grow, despite frequent beheadings from the clanking guillotine lawn mower" (BH, 1). Although this figure is an attempt to sustain the metaphor of the "crusader's embattled fortress" several sentences before, the awkwardness in using the noun "guillotine" as adjective marks a hurried invention rather than a crafted fluidity.

The oral aspects of the book, that is the ways in which Vanessa the narrator writes as her characters are shown to speak, serve as implicit recognition of the knowledge that is unspoken, and unspeakable. Vanessa's childhood is a record of overhearing a laconic restricted code. The "long silence" (BH, 96) of the Métis in history, Piquette's lack of words, or her communication in curses, the cry of the loon, the silent stolidity of Chris's family—all these have unworded meanings with which the potentially verbose Vanessa must come to terms. She recognizes the power of her grandfather on his rocking chair, speaking "a kind of sub-verbal Esperanto" (BH, 51). Although it's not explicit in the novel, we can assume that Vanessa's story is in great part a release for someone who has had to avoid self-expression and curb angry words in an environment that makes guarded expression or silence a virtue. Nowhere is this ambivalence about talk more strikingly embodied in the novel than in the account of her father's death in "A Bird in the House." Vanessa jumps from describing embracing her mother to describing "the days following my father's death" (BH, 91) without ever explicitly telling us that her father died, or how, or when, or why. This revealing suggestion of the child's point of view is at the same time gripped by puritan reticence. When years after her father's death she finds a hint that during the war he might have had a secret love, she laments: "Now that we might have talked together, it was many years too late" (BH, 95). If the style of Vanessa's narration is some kind of "talking together," then it may contain this ambivalence: she is both giving voice to what was unexpressed in her childhood, and, crucially, acknowledging the power of a relationship in which things must go unspoken.

In other words, style, in the sense of obvious literary device, is much less evident in Laurence than in Munro, reflecting Laurence's respect for the validity of the thoughts and ideas of, for example, someone like Piquette. Furthermore, the absence of overt technical devices (such as the Memorybank Movies in The Diviners) is more obvious here than in any of Laurence's other novels, perhaps reflecting this book's special interest in the child, whose own language is relatively restricted. Thus, in her syntax, Laurence uses occasional elisions and spoken tags to mark her commitment to a conversational mode. Similarly she slips into the free indirect style—"The parade would be almost over by now" (*BH*, 75)—indicating that the reminiscence is valid for the time referred to in the story.[14] And both syntactical forms also appear to reinforce the child's point of view; when Laurence writes of Uncle Dan, "He sang it very Irish" (*BH*, 24), she suggests the speaking voice recorded, as well as a touch of child grammar. But this is a child learning to be a writer, a lover of poetry, and, at least in her younger days, somewhat of a tyrant about grammatical rules she has learned (*BH*, 9). This side of Vanessa emerges, to be sure, from time to time, as if she has unwillingly let the inflexibility of the motto govern her own grammar: "we would go slithering and swooping across the floor in *whomever's* arms" (*BH*, 168; my italics).

Laurence also sensitively exploits the child's inability to comprehend metaphor. Vanessa's mother tells her " 'you've got your Grandfather MacLeod's hands and ears—.' " Vanessa remembers that "when I was younger, I had thought that my Grandfather MacLeod, who died a year after I was born, must have spent the last twelve months of his life deaf and handless" (*BH*, 26). This manifestation of the child's literalness in the face of metaphor might be merely cute or embarrassing, except that, thus remembered by the narrating Vanessa, the experience is perhaps a lesson in interpretation. In looking for, or in being sensitive to, the literal basis of metaphor in sensory experience, the adult writer, *locutor*, is inevitably going to be cautious about the necessity of the metaphoric flights she might be tempted to take in her own telling.[15] Or she might recognize the value of the worn metaphors which permeate a restricted code. Hence she tries, perhaps, in her telling, to rescue ordinary conversation from rote meaninglessness, as she clearly tries to bring ordinary experience into meaningfulness.

Lives of Girls and Women is, on one plane, much more densely detailed about the ordinariness—the diet, the dress, the interiors—of Del's childhood town. Yet attention to the verbal forms of Del's childhood, and to their potential reflection in Munro's style, suggests a very different emphasis. Whereas Laurence shows the significance of the ordinary, Munro experiments with the transformation of the ordinary. I have proposed that the primary grammars in Vanessa's childhood are kitchen dialogue, ballad or hymn, and motto. In Del's childhood the equivalent grammars are, probably, local history, operetta and the tabloid. Munro gives us much less banal dialogue, but she does quote long passages of direct speech, a convention which perhaps turns attention to the phenomenal memory of the narrator and which certainly allows for many characters to expand upon their own stories. Where songs appear in *Lives of Girls and Women* they function less to reveal character than to authenticate setting. Del hears stories in the songs; the last hymn in the novel is, aptly, "*I love to tell the story*" (*LGW*, 177). As for mottoes, they are at the edge of Del's experience (*LGW*, 148). Munro, we might venture, is more a creator of mottoes; her writing often approaches the aphorism that elegantly catches a fine distinction, a phrase that might become an epigraph.

Uncle Craig's history of Wawanash County is an uncompleted account of "daily life," a record of "public events," "a great accumulation of the most ordinary facts" (*LGW*, 26-27). Local history is not a form of narrative which either the young Del or the grown narrator find congenial. Except for freaky stories, such as one telling of Jenkin's Bend being named "after a young man killed by a falling tree" (*LGW*, 25), Del finds Uncle Craig's history a product of "masculine self-centeredness" and, especially, a doomed attempt "not [to] leave anything out" (*LGW*, 26-27). After Uncle Craig dies, Del inherits the manuscript and her aunt's dream that she would finish it. But Uncle Craig's crude transitions, and avoidance of story, have no appeal to a writer interested only in "a masterpiece" (*LGW*, 52), and she is more relieved than guilty when the manuscript is destroyed in a flooded cellar. Although she deliberately avoids Uncle Craig's kind of narrative, Del cannot, it seems, avoid the same temptations. As she admits to herself in the "Epilogue," she is something of a photographer, with an obsession for lists. Uncle Craig's obsessiveness is surely reflected in her own syntax. For the young Del, "learning a list of facts was an irresistible test" (*LGW*, 56). Against that categorizing grammar is the more attractive form of multiple stories. These can broadly be divided into the narrative of operetta (including opera and theatre) and the narrative of the tabloid (including, in this work, elements of the gothic romance).

Story is rampant in this novel. Uncle Benny tells stories, Auntie Elspeth and Auntie Grace tell stories, Fern and Del's mother pass their time together telling stories. Uncle Bill is a storyteller, as is Mr. Chamberlain, and the unlikely Garnet French. Even Jerry Storey who, despite his name, detests fiction, is not beyond turning facts "into a Great Comic Scene" (*LGW*, 171). A character who is not a storyteller, like Del's father, is a rarity and has little place in Del's life. Jubilee takes its whole existence from story. This carnival of accumulation, more than any other element, establishes the child world in the novel, despite the judging adult retrospective I have described. At one level, Munro's form creates an impression of frenzied confusion, a kind of self-absorbed autistic construct. As we are told, in Jubilee "reading books was . . . a habit to be abandoned"; to be immersed in story, even oral story, is to remain outside the "seriousness and satisfactions of adult life" (*LGW*, 99). In the child's being "drawn . . . to . . . a dark sea, a towering whale, in a book of fairy stories" (*LGW*, 150), in the child's shaping her experience in these terms, Munro finds her child language.

Munro makes the production of the school operetta the pivotal incident in the development of her novel. In the operetta the ordinary small town of Jubilee gives itself over to the storied world suggested by its name. Of *The Pied Piper*, Del writes, "I was moved by the story, and still am" (*LGW*, 110). In the world of the story she finds freedom, a different, more egalitarian, more comradely, relationship between boys and girls is realized. Furthermore, only within the world of story is Del able to understand and appreciate other people: "I saw for the first time what he [Frank Wales] was like, what he looked like—" (*LGW*, 110). The lives of girls, at least, are contained in the operetta seen through a child's eyes. The magnification, the exaggeration, the fantastic, even the grotesque are seemingly things to be clung to. The "theatrical in religion," expressed in "the most elegant channels of language," is the greatest pleasure for Del. Thus, her impulse is always to place "the richness of the words against the poverty of the place" (*LGW*, 83).

Del tends to see her life in melodramatic terms, from the "slim young green" frogs that she "squished . . . tenderly" in her hands (*LGW*, 1), to the "absurdity and horror" of her "Baptizing" (*LGW*, 198). On the one hand, a decided tabloid mentality governs Jubilee, her mother, and the grotesqueness of the stories she hears. But, more important, when Del tells stories herself, her selection of incidents, her syntax, her literary devices seem often to reflect her early fascination with the "versatility and grand invention and horrific playfulness" (*LGW*, 4) of the tabloid newspaper. (The tabloid's emphasis on photographs is also, surely, more than accidental.) Certain dominant features of child narrative provide interesting parallels here: the heavy use of "gratuitous terms" and "stressors" in children's storytelling may make the operetta particularly attractive. And the child's lack of attention to orientation and context, her tendency to end at the high point, seems to reflect the tabloid's method.[16] It's as if Del, like many of Dickens's children, is caught in the magnified, distorted story of the tabloid and can't quite escape, despite the claims of fact and logic. This attraction, I would argue, puts the central character in a slightly absurd position, which is particularly attractive to Munro. Del looks on her childhood as a rather bizarre, if attractive, distortion.

Against the Baptist blandness of Jubilee's surface, Del places the exaggerated sensitivity of the operetta and the reckless speculativeness of the tabloid story. Startling transitions and grandiose diction imply the sensational. She prefers the incongruously sophisticated expression, say her mother's "virginal brusqueness" (*LGW*, 150), or the "iridescent brooch" (*LGW*, 37) of flies on the dead cow. The sophistication of Munro's diction is admirably explicated by Helen Hoy in an article which examines "the centrality of paradox and the ironic juxtaposition of apparently incompatible terms or judgements" in Munro's fiction. One effect of Munro's compact paradoxes, Hoy argues, is to convey "the intense emotional ambivalence of adolescence."[17] I agree, and would particularly emphasize Hoy's awareness of a "bizarre" absurdity which is consistent with the grammar of operetta and tabloid throughout *Lives of Girls and Women*. It may be worth noting in this context that a noticeable feature of early speech is "the frequent confusion of antonyms . . . which suggests that the child grasps the dimension of space or action or feeling defined by an antonym before the polar extremes are clearly differentiated."[18] Perhaps some of the paradox in Munro evokes not only the grand extremes of tabloid story, but also this confusion in child language.

In the frenzy of implausible lists and Grade 7 metaphors Del seems to be placing herself self-consciously as some slightly absurd misfit. In "Baptizing," for example, she describes the June night, with "the sky like a peach skin behind the black pines" (*LGW*, 155). Just how far the reader should pursue such an analogy is always uncertain, but, as with the memories of child language, Munro seems to be more than slightly ironic here. Such irony is tellingly suggested by the "Epilogue," in which Del mocks her own style by burlesquing such metaphors, showing them to be rather superficially applied, as in a Farris/Boyce operetta, rather than thoroughly thought through: she discusses Caroline, one of the characters in her own imagined novel, "her *bittersweet flesh, the color of peeled almonds*, burned men down quickly" (*LGW*, 204). This feature of Munro's style needs much fuller examination. But, I would suggest here that Del's sense of story dictates metaphor for instant effect, not for multiple resonance, just as in the world of tabloid, and operetta (and childhood), the metaphors are based on the perception of but a *single* association between the objects compared.[19]

In order to sum up the child languages in Munro and Laurence I want to end where I began, with paired passages of evident narrative and thematic similarity, but of noticeable difference in approach. If Vanessa MacLeod speaks in something resembling a restricted code, Del Jordan's letter-writing mother, with her "somehow noticeable use of good grammar" is certainly the possessor of an elaborated code, "analytic . . . generalizing, transforming [her] immediate experience into philosophical gestures."[20] Ironically, though her mother is such an embarrassment in the "long decorative descriptions" she uses under the Tennysonian "nom de plume *Princess Ida*" (*LGW*, 68), Del recognizes something appealing both in her "innocence" (which reminds her constantly of resuscitating her "younger selves" [*LGW*, 62]) and in her need to say something "remarkable" (*LGW*, 68): "I myself was not so different from my mother, but concealed it,

knowing what dangers there were" (*LGW*, 68). An obvious result of her
mother's influence is that Del comes to think and write in the "highly
symbolic and emotionally expressive language of literary Romanticism."[21]
As the following parallel passages show, Del's writerly code expresses some
of the innocence of her loner mother, whereas Vanessa's restricted code at
once validates her child language and marks a mature sense of community
commitment:

> He looked exactly the same as he had in life. The same handsome
> eagle-like features. His eyes were closed. It was only when I noticed the
> closed eyes that I knew that the blue ice of his stare would never blaze
> again. I was not sorry that he was dead. I was only surprised. Perhaps I
> had really imagined that he was immortal. Perhaps he even was
> immortal, in ways which it would take me half a lifetime to comprehend.
>
> (*BH*, 177)

> The bottom half of Uncle Craig was covered with a polished lid; the top
> half—from shoulders to waist—was hidden by lilies. Against all that
> white his face was copper-colored, disdainful. He did not look asleep;
> he did not look anything like he looked when I went into the office to
> wake him up on a Sunday afternoon. The eyelids lay too lightly on his
> eyes, the grooves and creases on his face had grown too shallow. He
> himself was wiped out; this face was like a delicate mask of skin,
> varnished, and laid over the real face—or over nothing at all, ready to
> crack when you poked a finger into it.
>
> (*LGW*, 49)

The Laurence passage has eight sentences averaging eleven words each; the
Munro passage has five sentences averaging twenty-three words each. Yet
even this startling difference is less marked than it might be if I had included
more of the context for the quotations. Only the first three of Laurence's
sentences describe the physical appearance of her grandfather in death.
Munro's description is excerpted from a still fuller account of Uncle Craig's
appearance, and, indeed, from a lengthy story within "Heirs of the Living
Body" focusing on the young Del's reluctance to look on the dead body.
    Clearly Munro uses a more complicated syntax and a less neutral
vocabulary than Laurence. In *Lives of Girls and Women* the language
analyzes the reaction of young Del which it presents. Del seems to be
crafting a story about a character who only distantly resembles her adult
self. In *A Bird in the House*, the language, although the Vanessa
remembered is here twenty years of age, works to preserve the naive
perception of a much younger self, defying, perhaps, the symmetrical

proprieties of the puritan adult she is intended to be. Vanessa seems to be recorded reminiscing aloud, in shifting tenses, about the connections between the child she was and the person she is.

The Munro passage is relatively rich in adjectives (implying judgements) and in modifying prepositional phrases (13). The occasional modifiers that Laurence does use—"exactly," "handsome"—are relatively neutral, almost blank and automatic. Both use mainly linking verbs but Munro uses three passives which distance Del from the remembered experience, quite differently from the relationship in Vanessa's account. Vanessa's personal involvement is implicit in six first-person pronouns, where the Munro passage has only one. Laurence's shorter and simpler sentences, including one sentence fragment, suggest the rhythm and hesitation of oral presentations.[22] It is easy to imagine this passage being performed on stage, the periods signalling pause for effect and consideration. The most noticeable metaphor in Vanessa's undecorated description is her memory of the "ice" of her grandfather's stare. That this is remembered as "blazing," and is therefore a mixed metaphor, again identifies a casualness of presentation. In this case, as well, the "literariness" of the metaphor is also undercut by the colloquial syntax: the formula "It was . . . that," adds several words unnecessary to the meaning. The same not quite fully considered word selection might be found in the paradoxical phrase "really imagined" where, as in the restricted code, the reader is expected to understand the speaker, not examine the semantics.

Del/Munro seems to calculate her effect carefully, distancing herself so that the reaction is more in the reader than the character. The use of the passive voice is one distancing device in this passage, fewer uses of the first-person pronoun another. More significantly, the similes, rather than suggesting the young Del's perception, are so carefully elaborated and extended—the comparison of face to mask takes twenty-eight words—that the reader is impressed by the innocence of a scrupulously articulated revulsion, expressing the writer's discovery, rather than by the intensity of Del's reaction as child.

In short, one might think of Del as indulging in the role of Romantic innocent, but not as naive (as one thinks of Brian O'Connal, or Emily Carr's Small, or Vanessa). She always seems capable, even when the earliest memories are her subject, of considered, elegant insight. Such is the effect of multiple modifiers, and of the more complicated syntax, the compound-complex sentences, of beginning the second sentence in this passage with an adverbial phrase. Perhaps most interesting are the balanced doublets which appear everywhere in Munro's style, a feature obviously consistent with Hoy's emphasis on paradox in Munro. "The bottom half" of Uncle Craig is balanced with his "top half." The image of "copper" is balanced with the evaluative abstraction "disdainful." Of these five sentences four are compounded, not by "and," but by juxtaposition through semicolon or comma splice. Thus the discriminations suggested by the balance in the title, the equivalent stories suspended through the book, and a syntax which consistently gives equal weight to apparently competing observations, imply the shrewd considerations and adjustments of a finely tuned, sensitive mind.

The forms of discourse that govern Vanessa's childhood are participatory—they require community articulation. Del's childhood is shaped by forms of discourse which imply audience, spectators—they are forms to be watched, perhaps sceptically. In Laurence's novel we share the sense that it is possible to know something without realizing it: there is a knowledge beyond language, and one mark of Vanessa's maturing is to recognize that possibility, as it was often contained in her own childhood. In Munro's novel, the language of childhood is the language of children's story, or of the stories Del hears as a child. Del is always seeking "the relief of making what Mr. Chamberlain had done into a funny, though horrifying, story" (*LGW*, 144). In that tendency, we confront, uneasily, the possibility that the "lives," in the sense of the biographies or stories, of girls and women are at once the same. That is a political comment. As is the narrator's implied discovery that the "lives" must be different: the lives of girls shaped by the male centred 'realism' of local history, the sentimental romance of operetta, and the violence of tabloid, must not be the lives of women. In one way and another both Laurence and Munro attempt to create a fictional form which will give convincing articulation to that conviction.

3

Perpetual Rebeginnings:
The Short Fictions of Clark Blaise

Indeed it is not unusual for the memory to condense into a single mythic moment the contingencies and perpetual rebeginnings of an individual human history.

> Sartre, SAINT GENET

I had overcome my false starts and had begun to accumulate a personal history. Suddenly I had no evidence of a personal history. It was a kind of freedom that depressed me profoundly.

> Clark Blaise, DAYS AND NIGHTS IN
> CALCUTTA

The first of these epigraphs prefaces the third section of Clark Blaise's *A North American Education*. Blaise is very fond of epigraphs, themselves a condensing, a way to begin, or, because they place the text in a new perspective, a rebeginning. And a partiality for epigraphs is one feature of the rhetoric of rebeginning to which Blaise, through the quotation from Sartre, directs us. The structures, large and small, of his short fictions have the rhythm of compounded epigraphs. Individual sentences and phrases are typically aphoristic, separable, quotable in isolation. Each complete piece seems to move haltingly through an assembly of passages any one of which might be prefix or preface. "Contingencies" and "perpetual rebeginnings" are the essence of the lives of Blaise's characters; a memory creating "mythic moments" suggests—elliptically—his narrative technique. The narrating memory is continually searching childhood for the defining incident. Yet for all the importance of childhood in Blaise's fiction, its associations are less with the vividly fresh perception of discovery than with profoundly depressing freedom. If there is a vivid present in most Blaise stories, it is the moment of bewilderment in the searching memory as it encounters the confusion of a child beginning. As the second epigraph demonstrates, the sensation of a disappearing history is pervasive enough even to shape the persona of an autobiographical travel journal.

To describe the form and style through which the writer authenticates the child's experience in *A North American Education* and *Tribal Justice* poses a quite different problem from, for example, the stories of Margaret Laurence, or Alice Munro, from *Huckleberry Finn* or *David Copperfield*. Although Blaise's central character is usually a young boy (never a girl), often a pre-adolescent, and although Blaise is capable of sensitive recreations of the child's encounter with the world, it is not the story of the child, of his growing up, or the consciousness of an individual child *per se* which holds the two collections together. What does hold them together is a child language of perpetual rebeginnings. That is, Blaise's characters, whether literally children, or middle-aged, are forever starting over: reading about them is like reading a group of self-contained segments which are aslant to a potential narrative that never quite emerges. In this context the specific markers of hesitant rebeginning—that is, the distinguishing features of Blaise's child language— are found not so much in the early stages of language acquisition as in occasional unexpected deviations from syntactical norms, especially in a peculiar preference for infinitives. Child language in Blaise repeatedly identifies the child character's awkward beginning with the adult's puzzled rebeginning. His interest is not so much in child characters as in a state of awareness, a state of rebeginning, for which childhood is the most obvious analogy.

A child's world, that is, obviously involves beginnings and first encounters; relative to it the adult's world has stopped expanding and involves more repetition, more encountering the familiar.[1] In this sense, Blaise's stories stumble through a child's world, a world where the child is always moving to a different home, at the extreme "every week or two" (*NAE*, 225). As the narrator exults in "Eyes": "You're wandering happily, glad that you moved, you've rediscovered the innocence of starting over" (*NAE*, 21). But the experience is not so enriching as this quotation, out of context, might suggest. Physical dislocation results in emotional and psychic dislocation. Starting over implies plunging again into confusion and bewilderment: never feeling at home, never learning, never building. The innocence "of starting over" is more the sort we associate with the Jamesian child: as Peter Coveney describes it, a "painful capacity for impression and sensation, for corruption, for, above all, becoming the victim."[2]

Certainly Blaise's children live in a world of much pain, often touched by a particularly gruesome, all-engulfing, senseless brutality. In "Words for Winter" the six-year-old Greek boy, Nikos, falls to his death from a second-floor balcony: "he flashed silently across my vision, a white shirt striking the muddy yard with a whip-sharp crack" (*NAE*, 33). To the narrator, Norman Dyer, the violence is somehow absurd. He can't get it into any kind of perspective. Similarly, "Going to India" begins incongruously with a "horror story" of a boy going over Niagara Falls on a raft: "Children in Niagara country must have nightmares of the Falls, must feel the earth rumbling beneath them, their pillows turning to water" (*NAE*, 59). Children in Blaise country do have such nightmares. Frankie Thibidault, in a grotesquely bloody scene, is knocked off his bike by a catgut line strung across the road by his classmates. His life, analogous to that of each Blaise persona, is lived with the constant awareness that "something dreadful could suddenly cut him down without warning" (*NAE*, 194).

When any road through one's childhood might have catgut strung across it, the memories are something to be "scream[ed] . . . out of existence."[3] Blaise's typical narrator can not avoid remembering, but the mythic moments are more to be avoided than embraced. In one story, "The March," the narrator admits that memories are an addiction, "*especially* the imperfect ones" (*TJ*, 130; my italics). Remembering is not a means of integrating and understanding (as it is, say, in Wordsworth), but an obligation to begin again, uneasily, at another point of groping in an unrecognizeable world. Something of the function of memory in Blaise is nicely expressed in a poem by William Carlos Williams:

> Memory is a kind
> of accomplishment,
> a sort of renewal
> even
> an initiation, since the spaces it opens are new places
> inhabited by hordes
> heretofore unrealized.[4]

Memory in Blaise, in contrast to the sense of continuity it establishes for Laurence's Vanessa, does not lead us to comfortable and familiar places, but to "new places" and to encounters with "hordes: heretofore unrealized."

The very young child, too, is in a "new place," with no language, no sense of identity, surrounded, in William James's famous phrase, by a booming confusion. The adult returns to a similar situation in the giggling helplessness of trying to learn another language, in being an immigrant, in being a tourist in a strange city, uncertain of directions, puzzled by names, nervous, unsettled, frightened. If this condition were the focus in a few

Blaise stories, it would hardly deserve extended comment. But the thematic preoccupation, "perpetual rebeginnings," is also a key, in several senses, to the narrative forms of Blaise's short fictions.

First because, as I have mentioned, Blaise's basic 'plot' describes continual moving, not wandering for its own sake, but repeatedly trying to settle again in a new place. This pattern of ceaseless moving is summarized in "The Salesman's Son Grows Older":

> The loss, the loss! To leave Montreal for places like Georgia and Florida; to leave Florida for Saskatchewan; to leave the prairies for places like Cincinnati and Pittsburgh and, finally, to stumble back to Montreal a middle-class American from a broken home, after years of pointless suffering had promised so much. (*NAE*, 155)

So Frankie Thibidault sums up his life, a life in which he never quite catches up, never becomes a complete adult, never becomes civilized: he grows older, but he doesn't 'grow up.' The passage, consequently, is a good example of Blaise's child language. Recollection is blurred: memory does not frame past experiences or put them in perspective, but is an initiation. The syntax of the passage colours the subject in a significant way. The only predicate is in a subordinate clause. The potential motion of "leaving" —and "loss"—is stopped in nouns and noun phrases. In context the infinitive is a crucial marker of the child register: it is the most formless of verb forms, without indication of person, tense, mood—or of actor and action. Four infinitives in proximity mark a sensibility which is all potential—unformed, uncompleted. Although the infinitive is not the form the child would use, Blaise's example shows how it can function as an indicator of the child's experience. The sentences have a series of beginnings, but no endings. The same patterns shape the stories of Norman Dyer, immigrant surrounded by immigrants in Montreal, or of Paul Keeler, searching for "love and culture" through Europe and India. The various narrators carry different heritages—French-Canadian, English-Canadian, American—but they are living through the same experiences: they form a single personality, always at a loss, always stumbling. They are North Americans, uneasy in their occupation of space.

If constant removal is a basic condition in Blaise's stories, the experience conveys a curious stasis; it is not the exhilarating wandering so popular in American fiction. In "The March" such freedom tempts Pierre, but he never fully endorses it: "I'd read my Wolfe and Dreiser, and for the first time I let myself think that Wolfe had won the argument after all: flow, drift! Screw necessity! I saw nothing to contain me" (*TJ*, 150). Removal is not willed, but is dictated by some unchallengeable power—most likely by parents or economic necessity. Always an only child, always moving, Blaise's protagonist never finds a peer group; therefore he never grows through egalitarian relationships, or through comfortable independence from his parents, he does not learn about taboo subjects gradually, and he is totally out of touch with trends.[5] Thus distorted, Blaise's adult/child protagonists, despite a desire "to sink into the city, to challenge it like any other immigrant and go straight to its core" (*NAE*, 30), are arrogant, innocent, and without community. Not only is it absurd to think that moving into a roach-infested flat in an immigrant neighbourhood will bring authenticity, but the very desire to "challenge" this unfamiliar society seems perverse. The rootlessness has taken root; the characteristic protagonist in a Blaise story doesn't want to make a home, doesn't want to fit in.

The second pattern of rebeginnings in Blaise is less explicit than the geographical movement. Certain very specific situations recur in story after story. These are more than simple image motifs holding the various stories together. By putting the same situation in a different time, or place, or by seeing it from a different point of view, associating it with a different character, Blaise conveys a sense of 'let's begin that over again; that's not quite right.' The personless, timeless compounding of infinitive and participial constructions is echoed in the larger patterns of narrative (or non-narrative): "to leave," "to leave," "to leave" is to repeat an experience without getting anywhere. The list of recurring situations and images is lengthy: abandonment by a father, the dark half-discovery of a father's marital infidelity, the adolescent voyeur caught in fantasy and squalid reality, a plague of mice or cockroaches, the encounter with dentists (and the curious metaphorical association of dentists and winter), fishing, the smell and feel of camphor berries crushed underfoot, the sound of a skipping rope. In contrast to the sense of carnivalesque abundance which builds from lists and recurring experiences in Alice Munro's *Lives of Girls and Women*, Blaise's protagonists seem to be living the same story over and over.

In "Going to India," Paul Keeler remembers the "worms in my feet" (*NAE*, 64), an apparently random example of the discomfort of being a tourist in the Bahamas and Cuba. In "Broward Dowdy" the narrator finds his feet itching "maddeningly with tiny threadlike worms" (*TJ*, 4), a brief glimpse of initiation to a new home in rural Florida. But a few pages later, in "The Fabulous Eddie Brewster," a different narrator describes "foot worms" (*TJ*, 34) as a permanent condition of Florida's sticky ugliness. In "A North American Education" Frankie Thibidault remembers, at much greater length, the ritual of curing foot worms: the unsuccessful cure of the Florida doctor, the folk remedy of a slovenly neighbour, and especially the affliction as a sign of his maladjustment to the South. After his foot had peeled, the worms gone: "I thought . . . that in some small way I had become less northern" (*NAE*, 166). Four different people, all with foot worms at different times, in different southern places, with different significances—and yet, clearly, the same experience. Beneath the individual stories is a composite narrator who is rebeginning, caught in what Freud called the repetition compulsion: "the individual unconsciously arranges for variations of an original theme which he has not learned either to overcome or to live with."[6]

Being in a strange world, marked as an outsider by an incomprehensible, crawly affliction, conditions the Blaise child. Rebeginnings insist on being a framework for understanding. Blaise's protagonists are constantly thrown back to begin again at the stage of five-year-old Frankie Thibidault, at the stage Piaget called pre-operational, where thought is egocentric, where reason is dominated by perception, and where the only solutions to problems are intuitive rather than logical. One analogous situation for the adult is to be lost in an environment where no one speaks your language. It's a situation, of course, with extra resonance in a country with two official languages; more profoundly than afflictions with foot worms, experiences of another language give Blaise a formula for the confusion of rebeginning. Usually the appearance of a non-English word or phrase in Blaise does not extend or refine meaning (it's not used because an equivalent term does not exist in English) but signals a fumbling undeveloped language—to translate, to translate. Norman Dyer, perhaps condescendingly, observes his students' vulnerability with a new language: "French Canadians [are] like children learning the language" (*NAE*, 10). In "Continent of Strangers" the lack of language is traumatic; Paul Keeler is so innocent, so childlike, so nearly paralyzed in Sweden, as in Germany, that he dreams: " 'We'll go someplace else . . . somewhere I speak the language. England. France. I'm just not ready for someone to call '*Guten Morgen*' when I think I'm alone' " (*NAE*, 127). In "The March" Pierre eventually leaves his native Quebec, in part because he does not have complete control of his own first language: "In French, I'd remained a child" (*TJ*, 139).

The roles of salesman's son, always moving, and "student and teacher of languages" (*NAE*, 165), are closely allied. The literal and metaphorical rebeginnings figure in the ordering of the entire collection of fictions in *A North American Education*. The collection begins with a new beginning, with that "something fiercely elemental, almost existential, about teaching both his [Norman Dyer's] language and his literature in a foreign country" (*NAE*, 5), and ends with a beginning: "They'd be moving into the city that very night" (*NAE*, 230).

A fourth reflection of obsessive rebeginnings in Blaise's fictions is the self-contained units within some individual stories, such as "Going to India" and "Continent of Strangers." The parallel between such structures and the form of *A North American Education* as an integrated whole is particularly obvious in "Extractions and Contractions," where a collection of individually titled one- or two-page sketches makes up the complete piece. Building short fictions of even shorter, nearly discrete, segments is another way of structuring a series of beginnings. The form of rebeginnings is also continued in the play with chronology that is sometimes almost slipped by the reader. One striking example, in "A North American Education," is the crude and humiliating sideshow where young Thibidault spontaneously ejaculates in public. Several pages after the extended account of this incident, and without any clear indication that the chronology has been disrupted, the narrator tells us, "soon my father would take me to the county fair" (*NAE*, 182). This information comes as a surprise, and tantalizes, at least, with the possibility that we are to begin again, that the whole story will, or better could, be told again in a different way. Perhaps Frankie, even in retrospect, wants to think of the experience in a different way, wants to remember it differently. Memory is an "initiation," as Williams suggests, a beginning with "hordes/ . . . unrealized." The same strategy of memory as beginning occurs in "Snow People" where Frankie corrects his teacher's pronunciation of French-Canadian place names; this time, although the sequence of remembering is clearer to the reader, the story backtracks until we find that it would be "two years later when he rose to correct the teacher's pronunciation" (*NAE*, 204).

The notion of re-remembering implies the fundamental formal reflection of rebeginning which lies in Blaise's conception of fiction. Blaise considers his genre to be "short fictions," a form which can be distinguished from short *stories*. They are imaginings, reminiscent of Jorge Luis Borges' *ficciones*, bound not by logical organization, nor by chronological sequence, nor by cause and motive. They are, in their own way, reflections of the pre-operational sensibility, with the connections made more intuitively than rationally. Frank Davey gives a clear description of Blaise's characteristic concept, or method, of fiction. He notes the persistent lack of a central incident which would concentrate meaning, of a traditional climax. Davey links this form in several ways to the perspective of the innocent, though not to the idea of perpetual rebeginnings. His comment that "nothing can be climactic to one whose hold on the present is so tenuous"[7] is extremely germane to this argument. But I would reverse the point: the condition of beginning is to have only the present, the immediate sensation (Piaget stresses the importance to intellectual growth of acquiring the ability to conserve), without a sense of context in past and future. Despite constantly retrospective narrative, memory in Blaise's fiction brings precarious moments of present puzzlement, not understandings which can frame future action. For the Blaise character, it is not obsession with the past that causes a hold so tenuous, but his constantly beginning again.

An apt corroboration of the value of this approach to Blaise is found in the author's own comments on the art of the short story. In his commentary "To Begin, To Begin," published in *The Narrative Voice*, he gives three uses of the idea of beginning as a means of understanding fiction, *his* fiction. They are styled as advice to his reader:

> Lesson One: as in poetry, a good first sentence of prose implies its opposite. . . .
> Lesson Two: art wishes to begin, even more than end. . . . the ending is a contrivance . . . ; the beginning, however, is always a mystery. . . .
> Lesson Three: art wishes to begin *again*. The impulse is not only to finish, it is to capture. In the stories I admire, there is a sense of continuum disrupted, then re-established, and both the disruption and reordering are part of the *beginning* of a story.[8]

With the author's own suggestions as a guide, we can reflect at more length upon the energy of the beginning(s), and the sense of continuum disrupted.

"The Salesman's Son Grows Older" is usefully representative of the mystery of beginning—as theme and method—in Blaise's fiction. At age twenty-nine, the narrator, Franklin Thibidault, remembers the moves which, from age eight, have brought him to his present life in Montreal.[9] The fictional present, described at one point as "this long afternoon and evening," is scarcely defined at all: we don't know what he is doing, where, nor why this afternoon and evening seem "long." Yet this present moment, as disconnected from the past as it seems in many ways, is the centre of attention; we are interested in the salesman's son growing older. (One aspect of that interest is the vague sense of infidelity in love which might have brought Thibidault to his present beginning.) Interspersed throughout the fiction is a series of short reflections about the implications for himself and his son of the narrator's experiences. The structure of the story, defined typographically by spacing, is the series of moves: the night in Florida when Frankie and his mother hear that his travelling salesman father has been in a car accident; Frankie's stay with the near-strangers, the Davises, while his mother travels to Georgia; the preparations for moving; the week on the road on the way to Saskatchewan; the first summer in Saskatoon; that same October when his pen leaks into his mouth, he overhears that his father has another woman, and he is moved once again to an unnamed place; and a short, concluding section during which Frankie remembers his first year in Wisconsin.

Since Blaise urges that "in the first line . . . the story reveals its kinship to poetry"[10] we should look there for the sensibility behind (or, perhaps, created by) this series of moves. The salesman's son is introduced by a naturalistic detail, vividly remembered. We have to read two paragraphs before the narrator's relationship to this detail is hinted. "Twenty years later on a snowy night in Canada," he is remembering the peculiar "smell of a summer night in Florida": "Camphor berries popped underfoot on a night as hot and close as a faucet of sweat" (*NAE*, 142). This beginning signals an observer with a sense of the ugly and grotesque. He begins abruptly with memories of a sound, a physical sensation, and a pungent smell (camphor and sweat). The beginning, however, is not expository, but, lacking narrative context, mysterious. Throughout the story the proportion of visual images seems much lower than that usually associated with the master sense. Frankie's vivid memories are of hearing, touching, tasting, and smelling, rather than of *seeing* his world. Remembering his two weeks with Audrey Davis he can "still taste" the food, he can "still smell the outhouse and hear the hiss of a million maggots flashing silver down the hole" (*NAE*, 147). Even the frightening, and again mainly grotesque, visual image of Audrey Davis's breast—"nipple . . . poised like an ornament at its tip" (*NAE*, 147)—would be insignificant without the accompanying taste of kerosene and sugar, the quick touch of "fingertips over the hard, dry nipple and shafts of prickly hair" (*NAE*, 148). The effect of such concentrated emphasis on those senses which must operate at close range is to intensify the oppressive, "close" atmosphere of the story.

Thibidault's world is so oppressive because it is so self-centred. It seems, at any age, to be the unself-consciously egocentric world of the child. We receive only the sketchiest sense of any of the other characters in the story, including Thibidault's mother. Again, Blaise's narrator seems to be just at the vulnerable beginning of trying to adjust to his environment and establish relationships with the people in it, growing older without growing up.

Blaise's beginning is also appropriate to the uncertainly groping sensibility in a different way: the metaphor in the first sentence is fundamentally awkward. Certainly the "faucet of sweat" is vivid in its ugliness, but it is not apparently chosen to give insight either into heat or night. "Sweat" is neither particularly hot nor particularly close. That the faucet is the fixture, not what flows from it, reinforces our sense of encounter with a clumsy, crude personality. The impression is frequently conveyed in the Blaise metaphor: the striking first sentence of "Eyes" is both a mixed metaphor, and self-contradictory: "You jump into this business of a new country cautiously" (*NAE*, 16). As Frank Davey observes, in a comment on syntax which might also apply to metaphor, the narrator's "grip on [the] world is tentative and painful, much like his grip on the sentence."[11]

Blaise says the opening sentence "implies its opposite"; here the contrary implication is not immediately obvious. We find, of course, that the summer night in Florida implies the snowy night in Canada twenty years later. It also implies the summer of no sweat, the dry, burning heat of Saskatchewan, when we find Frankie, although still isolated, "as happy as I've ever been." But the more fundamental, instructive opposite is that the confined, stifled, awkwardness of the opening sentence describes the narrator's condition in the story's present; if, in looking back, he can sometimes conceive of himself, describe himself, as being in complete control, his *present* is a state of beginning over, in questioning bewilderment.

Frankie's memory is struggling to make something positive out of his childhood. He suggests, in the second paragraph, that the privileges of the salesman's son are uppermost in his mind, but almost everything we learn contradicts him. He lists the 'privileges':

> staying up late, keeping my mother company, being her confidant, behaving even at eight a good ten years older. And always wondering with her where my father was. Somewhere in his territory, anywhere from Raleigh to Shreveport. Another privilege of the salesman's son was knowing the cities and the routes between them. (*NAE*, 142-43)

The series of fragments itself suggests the narrator's uneasy lack of conviction; the privileges are dubious indeed, especially the privilege, for that is what the syntax clearly implies it is, of always wondering where his father is. In the next sentence, the reader is startled to be reminded that the narrator is still thinking of "another privilege," and is convinced only of Frankie's desperation to identify something positive about his childhood. Again the distancing memory is undermined by the immediacy of a child language. The sequence of gerunds signifies the absence of a sense of time—of date, of history, or of cause and effect. An impression of continuous but undifferentiated action is reinforced by beginning a sentence with "and." Even the last sentence, the only complete sentence in the passage, uses an "-ing" form as a near-echo of the formless beginning of the passage. And the syntax wobbles, even in the complete sentence, as if "privilege" is doing the knowing. It is just such slight deviations from the norm that give the sense of the loose grip on the sentence, and thus of the child's uneasy reaching for normalcy, for a coherence of beginning, middle and end.

If Frankie was indeed his mother's confidant, he remembers nothing that would convince us of it. The evidence asserts the reverse. On the night they receive news of his father's accident, he knows that after the neighbour women leave, he "would have to pretend to be asleep, or else go out and comfort her" (*NAE*, 147). But which he does, or whether he does *either*, his memory doesn't recount. The formless infinitives seem to usurp the syntax, to signal a child's confusion, which in this case is reinforced by the ambiguity of the parallel—could he *pretend* to go out and comfort her? When his mother returns from visiting his father in hospital, there is no communication between them: "I drew the conclusion that my father was dead, though I didn't ask" (*NAE*, 149). What Frankie does remember is that having a dead father brings a "deference, a near sympathy . . . that I'd been seeking all along and probably ever since" (*NAE*, 149). This is a rare moment when Thibidault has an insight into the reality of his present condition. He likes the condition of fragility which evokes the sympathy of others: as he says later, he knows "the role if not the words" (*NAE*, 160).

So the only child, near-orphan, lives a childhood defined by a series of sharply remembered incidents of absurdly embarrassing ineptness: huddling fearfully in a game of kick-the-can, isolated with an old *National Geographic* while his cousins luxuriate in physical labour, thrown to the floor by his teacher when his Hopalong Cassidy ballpoint leaks into his mouth. As in many other stories, his beginning over with language is made explicit: confronted in a new country with such words as "Saskatchewan hard," "bonspiel," and "skip," he decides not to say another word. In other cases, as with the opening sentence, the jumbled language is its own expression of vulnerability. When his humiliation with the leaky ballpoint is nearly complete, his mind fumbles irrationally:

> Worst of all you start laughing when you find I'm not dying. *But I am.* Stop it. You stupid Yank with your stupid pen and the stupid cowboy hat on top and you sucking it like a baby. I rolled to my knees. . . . (*NAE*, 157)

The deviant use of "you," with its apparently shifting referents, is another indicator of narrating memory becoming caught up in the confusions of a child language. This passage will completely confuse the reader, as surely as it expresses the confused bewilderment of the boy—then and in the narrative present. As Robert Lecker succinctly summarizes the relationship of teller and the "kaleidoscop[e]" of space and time in another Blaise story: "he is as unstable as his style."[12]

Memory's operations are themselves closer to the child's mental processes than to 'adult' reasoning, intellectual response. Memory is closer to dream, and fancy, than it is to logical understanding. In this story the details are very precise, but the total atmosphere is dream-like, as if the adult Thibidault is caught in a fantasy. This dreaminess extends to the narrator's present condition, revealed to us in brief passages of meditation that seem quite consistent with the boy frothing purply at the mouth. The most extended of these passages is the one chosen by the publishers of the paperback edition for the jacket blurb:

> My son sleeps so soundly. Over his bed, five license plates are hung, the
> last four from Quebec, the first from Wisconsin. Five years ago, when he
> was six months old, we left to take a bad job in Montreal, where I was
> born but had never visited. My parents had brought me to the U.S. when
> I was six months old. Canada was at war, America was neutral. America
> meant opportunity, freedom; Montreal meant ghettos, and insults. And
> so, loving our children, we murder them. Following the sun, the dollars,
> the peace-of-mind, we blind ourselves. Better to be a professor's son
> than a salesman's son—better a thousand times, I think—better to ski
> than to feed the mordant hounds, better to swim at a summer cottage
> than debase yourself in the septic mud. But what do these license plates
> mean? Endurance? Exile, cunning? Where will we all wind up, and
> how? (*NAE*, 155-56)

What this means, exactly, is no clearer to me than it is to Thibidault. I am
reduced, as he is, to a series of unanswered questions. Who is "We?" Why
did they leave Wisconsin? What was the "bad job?" Is it still bad? How does
"loving our children, we murder them" follow from the facile contrast
between the Canada and United States of twenty years earlier? Isn't the
rhetoric too extreme for the situation as we know it? What is the relationship
between murdered children and the son sleeping so soundly? What do these
licence plates mean? Conjunctions are rare; stock transitions are used
teasingly rather than helpfully. The passage begins by drawing the reader
into an apparently clear temporal framework. But with the phrase "and so"
(suggesting the child's first acquired, and then overused, conjunction?)
things start to slip. "So" implies a logical connection that can't be found.
Then, as they so often do in Blaise, a sequence of participles and infinitives
supplant the inflected verbs. The basic contrast between Thibidault as son,
and his child as son, repeatedly breaks down. We are not convinced that it is
better to be a professor's son than a salesman's son. We are sure that the
narrator is a son and not a father, that unlike Stephen Daedalus, whose
watchwords he echoes, he is still at a muddled beginning, that he has not
grown up.

   At the end of the story Thibidault briefly recalls a carefree childhood,
though it is not his own and is inaccessible to him. The writing is lyrical and
impressionistic, evidence of Blaise's shrewd use of language to evoke the
child's openness to sensation:

> I closed my eyes and heard sounds of my childhood: the skipping rope
> slaps a dusty street in a warm southern twilight. The bats are out, the

lightning bugs, the whip-poor-wills. I am the boy on yellow grass patting a hound, feeling him tremble under my touch. *Slap, slap*, a girl strains forward with her nose and shoulders, lets the rope *slap, slap, slap*, as she catches the rhythm before jumping in. (*NAE*, 160)

But the remembering is disconcerting: the rhythm and pattern of the game are beyond him. The startling shift to the present tense makes us realize what a distant observer of his own past Thibidault is. Blaise shifts to his own form of child language, so that rememberer, like child, seems to begin over without experience. The reiterated onomatopoetic word "slap" emphasizes sound pattern over meaning. The deviant elision of the article before "yellow grass," and the odd syntax of the second sentence, where two alternate subjects follow the completed kernel sentence, are other markers of Blaise's child's language. The boy on the grass is another person; to someone starting over, lost in the present, there is no connection. In the present there is repetition, but no learning. Each incident is in a vacuum. Another policeman at another door brings another apathetic, unthinking response. This last jumble of images and memories which will not cohere leads, somehow, to this mannered comment: "I'm still a young man, but many things have gone for good" (*NAE*, 161). This strange summation seems to be a realization of Blaise's own comment on story: "the ending is a contrivance." Thibidault contrives an ending, an ending which has a veneer of resolution about it, but which is essentially inconclusive. What things have gone it seems difficult to imagine: it seems certain that they are not things in his own character, or mind, or personality—not things which, in their passing, mark a growth, a stage in maturing. If anything is lost it is the external events, of the past—the teach-in, the policeman at the door, the girl skipping, the mangy dog, the boy on the yellow grass—leaving him suspended in the present, almost a child about to start over, and try to make some sense of the world.

4

Stages of Language and Learning in W. O. Mitchell's *Who Has Seen the Wind*

The child's world is the world, not of mountains, but of molehills; primarily not of steppes and prairies, but quite specifically of gardens. To name a flower is already to half-penetrate the secret of its world.

Richard Coe, WHEN THE GRASS WAS TALLER

In *Ox Bells and Fireflies* Ernest Buckler pauses to ask himself about the results of his public school education: "What kind of children did all this make of us?" And he answers: "Well, for the most part we were strangely adult. No Tom Sawyers."[1] Buckler is thinking particularly of the exclusion of pap or fantasy from his youthful reading. But his question raises a more fundamental consideration for his reader: it reiterates the problem, implicit at the beginning of the memoir, of the relationship between the narrator and the generalized boy "I" who is the book's subject, of the relationship between the author's deliberate remembering in a book and the time when "I did not think about any of it with these words."[2]

Recalling the time when the words weren't there emphasizes the apparent contradiction of trying to convey the child's simple, sensory, spontaneous encounter with the world through a deliberate and carefully worked language. Blaise tries to deal with the challenge by dwelling on the structures of beginning, both in syntax and narrative. Not surprisingly, many writers can only give us literary children who are "strangely adult," not in their actions, but in their feeling and thinking. "*Huckleberry Finn* as a whole, in its unique directness," notes Alfred Kazin, "makes us realize how little, elsewhere in American literature, children as themselves ever speak to us."[3] Certainly the author who writes a novel that begins with, and remains with, the life of a child (speaking or not) is very rare, and among these the number who have made a success of sensing and conveying the child's unique perception is smaller still. So any writer who approaches the task with a startling straightforwardness and humility—"This is the story of a boy and the wind"— must make a very special claim on our attention and on our hearts.

The story, of course, is W.O. Mitchell's *Who Has Seen the Wind* (1947), a novel unusual in its concentration on a boy's growing up during the pre-teenage years. When we think of Twain, and Tom Sawyer, and *Huckleberry Finn* (a novel to which *Who Has Seen the Wind* is often compared) we recognize other ways in which Mitchell's novel is uniquely focused. Because *Huckleberry Finn* is in the first person, it is more a story *by* a boy than *of* a boy; Huck is mainly an observer of the world and his comments on adult society and morality are essential to the novel's appeal to adult readers, while Brian O'Connal is an active participant in his world, engaging himself with it in a familiar pattern of responding, accommodating, learning, and growing. Unlike Huck, a solitary refugee from society, Brian belongs to a normal family and class structure in an ordinary small town and attends an ordinary school every day. But, perhaps most significantly, whereas Twain follows Huck on a journey down the Mississippi, Mitchell carefully marks out the phases of Brian's development in formal and thematic stages. The structure of *Who Has Seen the Wind*, in four distinct parts based on Brian at four different ages, is a way of focusing attention on Brian's development and of understanding its nature. In using this definite pattern Mitchell shows a kinship to the psychologist who, although he knows that a child's growth is an uninterrupted continuum, invents "stages" to make comprehension easier.

A short preface directs the reader to Mitchell's intent: his subject is the "struggle of a boy to understand . . . the ultimate meaning of the cycle of life." Following the deservedly famous opening description of essential prairie, we first see Brian or, more correctly, we see his tricycle, wheel askew, in the middle of the sidewalk. "The tricycle belonged to Brian Sean MacMurray O'Connal, the four-year-old son of Gerald O'Connal, druggist, and Maggie O'Connal."[4] Appropriately we meet Brian through one of his playthings. Also, we meet him at an age when the problem posed by language is particularly prominent:

> By age three, the child deals very well symbolically with his familiar pragmatic world. By about age four, he begins once more to find his language inadequate to his experience. . . . The older preschool child learns to try answering his own questions. Not that he gives up asking his parents—but his questions come increasingly after an attempt at a formulation of his own, in the form of hypotheses.[5]

Certainly Brian finds his experience constantly running ahead of his language, and his speech is full of questions. Indeed Brian's first spoken words in the novel are questions:

> "Can I have a tent like the baby has?"
> "Ye cannot. 'Tis bad enough having the baby ill without—"
> "Is he ill bad?" (5)

The first question shows Brian trying to relate his brother's sickness to his own play-world. His second question shows more perplexity than concern, and more jealous desire to keep his grandmother's attention than either.

At once we note Mitchell's adeptness at suggesting child language. On the one hand his psychology is sound: Brian picks up two words, "bad" and "ill," which his grandmother has just used, and tries to fit them into his own understanding. On the other hand his poetry is sure: Brian's question carries a Calvinistic hint of the inherent evil in sickness, which would not be found in the grammatically correct, "Is he very ill?" The child's diction is deftly evoked, without seeming cloying or merely cute. Elsewhere Brian says "belshes" for "belches" and "crissmus" for "Christening." Mitchell slips a child's coinage into his description here and there—"sunshiny," "clicketing"—to reinforce Brian's point of view. Brian, in short, is following the natural patterns of adapting the sounds, prosody and grammatical forms of the language. Again Mitchell is at his best when he discovers within this process a special sensory vividness beyond Brian's understanding; a startling and funny example is Brian's comment on his grandmother's illness: " 'She's got room-a-ticks in a leg' " (10).

We hear Brian trying to answer his own questions in passages where Mitchell nicely catches the humorous non-communicating nature of child dialogue:

> "Do you know anything more?" asked Brian.
> "I'm hungry. Maybe if you was to ask, your maw'd give us a piece."
> "The baby's going to heaven," explained Brian.
> "My Dad's a conductor," Forbsie said, "on the C.P.R. He has got silver buttons."
> "It's where God stays," said Brian, "heaven."
> "No it ain't," said Forbsie. (6)

Brian and, to a lesser extent, Forbsie, speak egocentrically without intending to communicate, as if they were thinking out loud. Brian's speech here is an accompaniment and reinforcement of his mental activity, a way of channelling his thoughts and, therefore, of exploring himself. In distinguishing such characteristics from adult language Piaget gives us one framework within which to consider Brian's development:

We may safely admit that children think and act more egocentrically than adults, that they share each other's intellectual life less than we do. True, when they are together they seem to talk to each other a great deal more than we do about what they are doing, but for the most part they are only talking to themselves. We, on the contrary, keep silent for longer about our action, but our talk is almost always socialized.[6]

Brian is a contemplative and reflective child, more so than most of his companions apparently, though we hardly know the others well enough to say. At any rate, Brian seems to have less and less to say as the novel proceeds. The implication is that (to use Piaget's pattern) as Brian grows to an age where speech becomes more and more socialized, less a tool for exploring the self, it becomes less essential to him. Yet Brian does become more committed to his family and to his community; he needs language for discovery, but he doesn't need talk to produce deep feelings for others.

Discovery involves trying to articulate his sense of the significance of the '' 'boy on the prairie' '' (24), or asking Digby the meaning of "engagement" (7-8), or, although he has been touched by the hand of the wind, asking Mrs. Hislop what a "spirit" is (9). In these and many other ways Brian is reaching for the language that will define his experience, change his experience, by giving him new channels through which experience may act upon him. So with the at first imagined, and then several times repeated, personalization of God as "R.W.," Brian finds an equivalent in language which allows him to hold onto a notion of God both as personally familiar and yet as slightly anonymous and deserving of great deference.

God is also the subject of the most fascinating example of child language in Part One, Brian's "song-one," a monologue in which he defines and explores his world while totally absorbed in a game:

"Now God is on a leaf—and the leaf is on a lawn—on a lawn—on a lawn—and He's got cuff links—He's got them on—on the lawn—and they are gold—they are gold cuff links—and they're yellow—so are the dandelions—and that's how God is—with gas on His stomach—with gas on His stomach—so He can belch if He wants to." (37)

Piaget describes how essential the monologue is to the child:

If the child talks even when he is alone as an accompaniment to his action, he can reverse the process and use words to bring about what the action of itself is powerless to do. Hence the habit of romancing or inventing, which consists in creating reality by words and magical language, in working on things by means of words alone, apart from any contact either with them or with persons.[7]

Song-one seems to be Brian's word for psalm, perhaps with a distant echo of solemn. Brian the singer is making poetry, that thing that "lies beyond seriousness, on that more primitive and original level where the child, the animal, the savage and the seer belong, in the region of dream, enchantment, ecstasy, laughter."[8] But again Mitchell's poetry contains a fine intuitive sense of child development, nicely expressing the connecting of single attributes of objects which characterizes the pre-school child's reasoning.[9] Brian is thinking from particular to particular, as a four-year-old must; the adult, overhearing Brian, recognizes the inherent concept of God: a playmate and friend, closely connected to natural things, yet set apart by the grown-up magnificence of gold cufflinks. Brian creates by words and magical language a God who is humanly fallible (suffering from a bit of gas), yet free to follow his own instincts. The serious side of Brian's song-one is emphasized by Mitchell's epigraph from Psalm 103, which also depends on images of grass, flowers and wind to express the relationship of man to God. Yet Brian's other model, "There's a frog on the bump on the log in the hole in the bottom of the sea," adds a sprightly sense of the interconnectedness of all things, expressing an enchanted wisdom beyond most adults in the novel.

Brian's experience may be running ahead of his language, yet language is enabling him, on a few occasions like this, to create and greet a reality which transcends concrete facts. At the end of Part One, when Brian first experiences that exquisite "feeling . . . of completion and culmination," it is an emotion, an instinct within him, which will only take on its full significance when he finds the language to fit it and explain it.

Part Two begins on 1 September 1931, Brian's first day of school. He is six years old; at the end of Part Two he is eight. In Piaget's terms these early school years are a period when a child's ways of thinking become less reliant on perception and intuition as he begins to think logically, at least about the world of real, concrete objects.[10] Mitchell, however, sees this stage of Brian's development dominated by a rather different factor:

like all children after the first blush of individuality at three, he was malleable and would remain so until perhaps the age of eight, when he would again try to impress his personality upon the world he had come to dissociate from himself. (89)

The passage reminds us that Mitchell is as interested in Brian's moral development as in his intellectual development. In his first years at school Brian's morality is determined largely by authority and by the approval of others. He is ruled, that is, by conventional morality; he is at a stage which a student of moral development, such as Lawrence Kohlberg, would see as typical of middle childhood.[11] Yet Mitchell's mention of an impending assertiveness suggests that in this, as in other areas, Brian is emerging as extraordinarily precocious.

Brian's questioning becomes more insistent at this age:

> "Why do people sleep, Dad?"
> Gerald O'Connal pursed his lips. "Habit."
> "What's that?"
> "Doing something over and over."
> "Well—why do you sleep over and over?"
> "You just do—while you sleep, you rest."
> "Can't a person rest without sleeping?"
> "Not as well," his father said. "When you sleep
> you rest better." (99)

These are questions more demanding of answers than the egocentric queries at the beginning of the novel. Piaget would call them "whys" of *motivation.*[12] Brian is looking not for the physiological cause of sleep but for the purpose or motive for sleep. His father intuits the direction of the question immediately: Brian is asking what makes people do the things they do.

Moments later Brian links his wondering about sleep to his continuing speculation about God: "Does God sleep?" Brian is once again considering the nature of spirit. But this time, instead of asking Mrs. Hislop for a definition, he is trying to formulate his own sense of spirit by looking for the link between God and his everyday experience. But hasn't this been Brian's direction from the beginning? Not quite. He is now specifically interested in a connection which will help him comprehend; he is approaching an awareness, therefore, that the two things are different in kind. This approach differs from the exuberant confidence of: "When God ate His porridge He had a dish as big as the prairie" (21). Whatever this analogy may be to the adult reader, it is literal realism for Brian. But now, in Part Two, he is increasingly, however tentatively, attracted to metaphor to bring understanding: "God could be like a flame, Brian was thinking, not a real flame, but like a flame" (99). The language here is covert and therefore not so firmly planted as to represent a conviction, but it certainly belongs to Brian. And in looking for the metaphor, then reminding himself that the flame would not be a real flame, Brian is logically seeking connections within his immediate, concrete world. He is using separate levels of reality, though he is not yet aware of it.

The trickiness of expressing the child's point of view is still clearer in another of Brian's metaphors:[13]

> The Catholic church bell began slowly and majestically to tongue the silence. Like on a lawn, he thought, with the inarticulate yearning in him deepening, a kid turning slow somersaults over a lawn—looking up with his head, then ducking it to take another slow turn completely over on the lawn. (107)

Here Mitchell is describing Brian's experience moments before that "turning point in Brian's spiritual life" brought on by his contemplating the dew drop on the spirea. The trick comes in slipping so easily from the narrator's slightly archaic rhetoric—"majestically to tongue the silence"—and its sense of the ancient grandeur of the established church, to Brian's vividly pictorial playground analogy. Not only is this second sentence a marvellous example of prose rhythm echoing sense, but it shows Brian again making something intangible (the bell's sound, but perhaps spirit and God are implied as well) available through tangible experience. This use of metaphor depends on his increasing ability to handle language: his comparison of the sacred tolling of the bell with the spirit of a child's game re-establishes that ancient link between ritual and play through their common elements— "order, tension, movement, change, solemnity, rhythm, rapture."[14] "Over a lawn, over a lawn, and over a lawn" (110) is Brian's personal version of "holy, holy, holy." This time the link is established not through chanting aloud to himself but through internalized language. Mitchell has pointed the development neatly by moving from the "song-one"—" 'God is on a leaf' "—to the "twinkling of light" on each leaf of the spirea. Brian is grasping the different levels of reality and reaching for their connection in the very midst of "an inarticulate yearning" for he knows not what.

We know that Brian has the Bible and the *Book of Knowledge* close at hand, but there is little evidence that he spends much time reading. Of course, book learning is presumably more important to Brian than its actual appearance in the novel indicates. Brian seems more impressed by the language which resembles his own "song-one." As a language to learn, Uncle Sean's poetic curses and Saint Sammy's harangues are particularly fascinating. Brian is mesmerized by their uneducated (in the formal sense), oracular, and playful use of language.

As a language to stimulate and extend his own thinking, the speech of the town's pop philosophers influences Brian much more than the discourse of the classroom. Joe, the drayman, for example, provokes him with the query " 'Wonder why a fella always has thoughts into his head?' "

> Brian had never thought of that; he'd never thought about thoughts before. Right now he wasn't thinking any thoughts; there wasn't any thinking going on in there. Yes, there was. He was thinking about not thinking; and he had just got done thinking about thinking about not thinking any thoughts, so he was thinking. Funny—boxes inside of boxes inside of boxes inside of boxes. (174)

Here Brian clearly moves beyond metaphor into the realm of purely abstract reasoning. It is a key development, preparing the way for the intellectual puzzling of the later sections of the novel. Brian's thinking about thinking contradicts Piaget's view that logical thought at this age is restricted to the concrete and perceivable. Uncle Sean's conventional expression of amazement, that the boys are " 'growin' up like stinkweed' " (116), takes on a new meaning here. Physical growth is the least of it; what is truly startling is the rate of Brian's intellectual growth. He is very advanced; a psychologist might even say, considering that at age eight Brian is three or four years young for such abstract thinking, that his precocity is impossible. At least there is some corroboration here for those readers who find Brian's reflections strangely adult. And we sense the difficulty that Mitchell faced in achieving a satisfactory thematic resolution through a pre-adolescent boy. But I look at these observations as ways of understanding the character of Brian, not as keys to flaws in the novel. First, to return to the subject of child *language*, we must note that Mitchell records Brian thinking, but Brian himself does not articulate the epistemological labyrinth. Brian will be capable of such thought, well before he can express the enigma. Moreover, so surely does Mitchell create a convincing sequence of development, so gradually does the process seem to unfold within the novel, that Brian's growth is convincing in the world of the fiction, however accelerated it may seem empirically.

Part Two sees Brian through the first two years of his schooling; Part Three opens in late July 1935 when Brian is "almost ten" (185). He is "lost in reflection," wondering about the meaning of "dog days" and thinking, again, about thinking:

> Hell!
> As soon as he had thought it, he wished that he hadn't. Sometimes thoughts could not be helped, for they were live and unpredictable things with hidden motivation of their own. *Damn* and *hell* were the livest of them all; they had a way of popping up full-blown and unbidden—not loud, but there in one's mind all the same. (187)

In many ways Brian is a very ordinary boy. But this interest in the process of thought reiterates how far apart he is from his peers. That the word *damn* in his mind is the livest of *thoughts* seem to emphasize the irony that as Mitchell moves toward confirming the power of feeling he must make Brian capable of abstract thinking beyond his years.

Having tried to define spirit, or God, through the sacred song-one in Part One and the playland metaphor in Part Two, Brian now has the use of secular literature in Part Three. The boys are still playing, but now within the more limited confines of reciting the Rossetti poem which gives the novel its title. Presumably they have had to memorize the poem in school:

> "Who has seen the wind?" Fat chanted.
> "Neither you nor I," returned Brian.
> "But when the trees bow down their heads—"
> "Nobody gives a damn," Art finished up. Fat laughed. (191)

In this exchange Brian, that most passionate asker of questions, is able to give the answer. Mitchell's title, significantly, omits the question mark, so that, although it contains the echo of a cosmic question, it also stands as a description of someone—Brian—who *has* seen the wind. Brian understands, to use Jung's definition, that "in keeping with its original wind-nature, spirit is always an active, winged, swift-moving being as well as that which vivifies, stimulates, incites, fires and inspires."[15] Although poem and question fascinate the boys, Art must detour the recitation lest they show, even among themselves, that worst of boyhood transgressions, love of learning. "Fat laughed," Mitchell says abruptly, leaving us to assume that Brian did not. He, we have already seen, does give a damn.

In fact he gives " 'Two million, five hundred thousand goddams' " (224) when he objects to the killing of the runt pig. Not only is this vigorous cursing Brian's most overt act of rebellion in the novel, not only is it an excellent demonstration of the rigidness of a young boy's emerging conscience (" 'killin' a thing's no favor!' " [225]), but it also confirms his kinship with Uncle Sean. Separated from his parents, brother, and friends because of his father's hospitalization, Brian is discovering "country," the endearing weakness of the cook, Annie, and the hidden gentleness of the severe evangelist, Ab. Now, as he "surprised himself with his fluency" (224), Brian adopts the lyric energy of his Uncle's cursing.[16] As with Sean's speech, this new-found fluency guarantees Brian's independence, his determination to think for himself, his passion for the land, and his respect for other people and creatures.

Undoubtedly Saint Sammy, that other curious loner and most exuberant curser in the novel, plays some part in Brian's new-found fluency. In Saint

Sammy, Brian finds someone who can carry him back to his four-year-old literal interpretation of God. For that delightful amalgam of King-James-version sonorousness and prairie-sod-buster slang is as significant a discovery for Brian as anything since the dew-drop on the spirea leaf:

> "To start with He give a flip to the fly-wheela thought, an' there was Heaven an' earth an' Him plumb in the middle. She had no shape ner nothin' on her." (197)

Shape is given to the thought, and creation occurs, through words; Brian, although he resists, realizes that the fervour of Saint Sammy's words has brought him closer to understanding than ever before. Yet Brian comes "alive . . . as never before" (199) by overhearing a chant "in a monotone, with the singsonging stress of a child's Christmas recitation" (197), which is intimately related to his own playful, and pre-semantic "song-one." Brian's excitement is intellectual: he is "passionate for the thing that slipped through the grasp of his understanding" (199). But behind the steady progress of Brian's intellectual development, Mitchell traces a counter-current which affirms the playful ecstasy of the four-year-old's approach to God.

Part Four begins almost two years after the death of Brian's father. The time is the spring of 1937; the novel has spanned the bleakest years of the Depression and drought from 1929 to 1937, as it follows the development of a boy from playful egocentric to concerned and contemplative youth on the verge of adolescence. Despite Mitchell's comic structure, with its impulse toward harmony, it is difficult to ignore that the Depression ends in the ecstatic ugliness of a world war, and that Brian's peace is about to be shattered by the storms of adolescence.

Brian's attraction to the Young Ben seems to intensify: "It was a taciturn association, almost a communication by silences" (253), as is the communication Brian has with the prairie. But even this communication, particularly his vision at the end of the novel, is made possible by his final and most crucial attempt to work out his understanding verbally. In the midst of the heady discussion between Digby and Palmer on Berkeley, Brian thinks of Saint Sammy and the feeling:

> "You got a feeling?"
> "Huh?"
> "You—do you get a funny feeling—like—well—you wanted to know something, only you don't know what you—Have you got a feeling?" . . .
> "It's like you are going to spill over," said Brian. "And you're all—"
> "No," said Mr. Palmer, "can't say I got that in there, kid. I got a

hell of a lot, but—I guess that ain't there no—more." He said it, thought Brian, sadly. (292)

However imprecise, this definition is Brian's most extended attempt to articulate the nature of his feeling. Feeling is not only a brimming of emotion and sensation but also, primarily, a hunger for knowledge, for ultimate knowledge. Faced with Brian's intellectualizing about feeling, with the impatient logic that goes beyond his years, Digby has to bring him back, in a sense, to his childhood, to accepting that everything doesn't necessarily have to "figure out." Understanding may come through feeling:

> "A person can do it by feeling?"
> "That's the way," said Digby.
> "Then, I'm on the right track." Brian said it with conviction. (294)

A short while later, just after his grandmother's death, Brian confides to Digby that he doesn't think he will get "the feeling" any more. Digby concludes that Brian has achieved "maturity in spite of the formlessness of childish features, wisdom without years. 'Intimations of Immortality,' he thought. 'Perhaps' said Digby to Brian, 'You've grown up' " (297). My consideration of Brian's development suggests several possibilities in Digby's qualifying "perhaps." Certainly Brian is intellectually precocious and is able in the last chapters to struggle with such a grand question as the ultimate meaning of life at a surprisingly young age. Similarly, his "new and warmer relationship with his mother" and his "growing consideration for the other members of the family" (251) suggest a moral development, a conception of individual rights, usually associated with adolescence. In Part Four Mitchell points to his father's death as a major influence on Brian's rapid maturing. Another important, if less explicit, influence is social and cultural. Just as Ernest Buckler's rural Calvinist background made "strangely adult" children, so a stern, small-town, prairie Presbyterianism pressured its children to hurry and grow up. In one of its dimensions *Who Has Seen the Wind* is a comment on a society too eager to put away childish things.

The other side of Digby's "perhaps" is obvious: at the end of the novel Brian is still a boy. So clearly and carefully does Mitchell examine the distinct stages of Brian's growing up that we must be very aware of the *next* stage as well. This next stage, of course, is adolescence, a period of sexual awakening, of strong peer pressure, and often of frustration and alienation. This awareness of impending adolescence causes some readers to find the novel, as I recall a student doing, "Disneyish." But Mitchell shows us many of the adult realities: the love triangle of Ruth Thompson, Peter Svarich, and Digby, the racial bigotry which drives Wong to suicide, the economic realities facing Sean when he tries to get a loan from Abercrombie, the pettiness of school board politics, and the frequent social and religious hypocrisy. These are things which have touched Brian scarcely at all. Their presence cannot be ignored; they put an ironic colouring on the novel, one which makes it more of, rather than less of, an adult novel. The same irony shimmers in the vision of prairie and cycles on the last two pages of the novel, an irony contained in such lyrically captivating phrases that it is often ignored. In its cycles the novel has moved from a sometimes bleak prairie June, to a snowy, grey prairie autumn. If we notice the "twilight" of the end of the novel, if we remember that the vision is of the light *and* dark, then we will not find the novel to be Disneyish but rather a more ironic view of the strength, and the implicit limitations, of the child's perspective.

Recalling Mark Twain's conclusion about conclusions in *Tom Sawyer* gives us some hint of what Mitchell must do:

> It being strictly a history of a *boy*, it must stop here; the story could not go much further without becoming the history of a *man*. When one writes a novel about grown people, he knows exactly where to stop— that is, with a marriage; but when he writes of juveniles, he must stop where he best can.[17]

As Mitchell tells us at the beginning, his novel is most assuredly a story about a boy. He can best stop, therefore, where Brian is no longer quite a child but is still a long way from being a man, where he can think of becoming a "dirt doctor" close to the soil and to the cerebral world of science, where the wholeness of the child's vision is still intact, where birth and death, love and hunger, can still be combined in a vision of unity and integrity, where awesome mystery is a feeling sufficient unto itself. Whatever adolescence and adulthood may bring, Brian will find "those obstinate questionings/Of sense and outward things . . . those first affections/Those shadowy recollections . . . Are yet a masterlight of all our seeing."[18] Digby's allusion to Wordsworth obliges us to see the final moment in the novel, as well as those many moments when Brian has the feeling, as intimations of immortality, as those moments "most frequent and compelling in unself-conscious childhood, moments when the soul, 'lost' to immediate selfish concern, catches a brief intimation of some ultimate pattern, a perdurable grandeur in the natural world or an elemental dignity in the human gesture."[19] But an awareness of the significance of such moments comes only, as it came to Wordsworth, in adulthood. Mitchell, ending his novel within the child's point of view, must give Brian adult ways of thinking in order to reveal the true value of those moments—such as his singing the "song-one" or hearing the church bell or trying to see the wind—which give a glimpse of the ultimate pattern.

5

Delight Without Judgement:
The Language of Visionary Enthusiasm
in Ernest Buckler's *The Mountain and the Valley*

*I have often encountered motifs which made me think that the unconscious
must be the world of the infinitesimally small . . . it seems to me . . . that
this liking for diminutives on the one hand and for superlatives—giants,
etc.—on the other is connected with the queer uncertainty of spatial and
temporal relations in the unconscious.*

Carl Jung

Toward the end of the Epilogue in *The Mountain and the Valley* (1952)
Ernest Buckler mentions, parenthetically, David Canaan's awe in the face of
" 'Nude Descending a Staircase' patterns."[1] In a novel some times valued
mainly for its nostalgic appeal, Marcel Duchamp's painting suggests the
modernity of Buckler's style and theme, and the geometric precision of his
structure. But the reference to "Nude Descending a Staircase" is particularly interesting since the painting provides an excellent image of Buckler's
difficult, multiplying style. Because Mitchell quotes Brian extensively, the
reader of *Who has Seen the Wind* is often tempted to consider the language
of the novel as a mimesis of children's speech. In *The Mountain and the
Valley* David rarely speaks; the language of the novel is studiously literary—
and, therefore, adult—but it contains frequent markers of the child's
sensibility.

Duchamp's famous painting stands out as an analogy for Buckler's
combination of scrupulously careful craft and breathless innocence: the
reference to Duchamp is one of a very few explicit indications of David's
learning, but the general absence of such references is, of course, an

important indicator of David as eternal child. We neither know where nor when David encountered the work, and its mention is not connected to any more general interest in modern art. On the other hand, cubism certainly provides a technique for representing rapidly swarming images at once imprinting themselves singly and blurring indistinguishably in the impressionable young mind.

Typically, the momentary thought of Duchamp's painting only intensifies David's wonder and bewilderment: "What is the mind of a man who would draw like that?" (296). In the same spirit, amazed and perplexed by Buckler's prose, I would vary the question only slightly: What is the meaning of a man who would write like that? *Like that*, more specifically, is the prose Claude Bissell describes as "the high metaphysical style,"[2] and which one of the readers of the manuscript judged, less kindly, "an uncontrollable spate of words"[3]—the prose which, according to Alan Young, contains "tortured sentences [that] make questionable demands upon a reader,"[4] and which Buckler himself feared might seem to be written by "a Thesaurusitic bastard."[5] Buckler is also, of course, quite capable of a plain style, for example in such narrative sections of the novel as the pig-killing, but I choose to concentrate on the exuberant style for two reasons: first, the occasional appearance of the plain style in *The Mountain and the Valley* only emphasizes more prominently the high style; and second, whatever else it may be, the plain style is certainly not David's style, although it may be the style David is looking for. Buckler presents us with many passages so compacted with meaning that they seem to contain the germ of the whole novel within them. Among the writers discussed in this book, Buckler confronts us most clearly with my continuing question: How can the most aggressively *literary* prose serve as a *child* language?

Because I am interested in Buckler's prose as it reflects or implies David Canaan's perception, I must leave aside detailed mention of the other characters although the novel continually emphasizes the closeness of the family. I will be emphasizing less the degree to which David changes and develops and more the extent to which he remains the same. Framed by the prologue and epilogue, in which David is thirty years old, *The Mountain and the Valley* follows David's development from age eleven, with occasional reminiscences of his earlier childhood. This pattern, and David's artistic sensibility, places the novel in the *Künstlerroman* tradition, and has focused critical attention on David's progress to adulthood. I find that an examination of Buckler's style, with its ironic indications of a non-rational even non-verbal understanding, forces a contrary emphasis on the ways in which David remains a child.[6]

The entire novel, for instance, is an answer to David's grandmother's question at the end of the prologue, "Where was David?" (18). In its literal

sense Ellen's question has only momentary interest: David has slipped out of
the house without telling his grandmother, and is on his way to the top of the
mountain. But her question is an ironic and resonant introduction to the
novel in the sense that it asks where David is within his own mind, and still
more importantly, in the sense that it asks what David's position is in time.
When, the question also implies, is David? Posed in this way, the question is
as important to David as to the reader. His angriest, his most disillusioned
moments—at the Christmas concert, in the pig-butchering scene, in the
argument with Joseph over moving the rock—centre on the insult of not
being quite a man. In Chapter 26, a year after David's fight with his father,
Buckler describes the subtle stages in a boy's growing up. Then he reminds
us, significantly just before Joseph again suggests going to the top of the
mountain, that "the conduit to childhood wasn't entirely sealed over. A
child's visionary enthusiasms still surprised you at times, trapped you into
delight without judgement" (173). This visionary enthusiasm, this sense of
being trapped in delight without judgement, strikes me again and again as I
examine Buckler's extravagant style. The conduit to childhood is open and
flowing freely. A parallel metaphor came to mind when I was rereading *The
Mountain and the Valley*, and I scribbled this note to myself: "Then, then,
methinks how sweetly flows/The liquefaction of his prose."[7] The allusion
still seems to catch the right sense of an act or process, of a prose line which
is so studiously precise, and yet which flows with the simple delights of
sound and movement. The essence of Buckler's fluidity is the list; his is the
aesthetic of getting-it-all-in, the spirit of exuberant profusion. An idea, as
David finds when he tries to write a story, will "frond suddenly like a
million-capillaried chart of the bloodstream" (260). To respond, the writer,
like Duchamp in "Nude Descending a Staircase," must superimpose a series
of slightly differentiated images, each geometrically fine in its accuracy, but
lost in the larger effect of sensuous movement where time is at once frozen
and non-existent. The sequence of slightly differentiated images, and the
thesaurus-like list of synonyms, are the central features of Buckler's child
language.

One such series of images describes the silence of an October twilight:

> As the light retreated, the silence sprang up with the same shivering
> stain the light had had. The feeding silence of the bluejay's dark sweep
> across the road . . . the partridge whirr . . . the straight flight of the
> dark crow against the deepening sky . . . the caution of the deer
> mincing out toward the orchard's edge . . . the caution of the hunter's
> foot on the dry leaf. And then the silence of the moment when the first
> faint urine smell of rotted leaves came from the earth, and the
> memory-smell of apples lain too long on the ground, and the sudden

camphor-breath that came from any shade stepped into, the moment the gun barrel first felt cooler than the gun's stock on the palm. The breath-suspending silence of the gun sight in the second of perfect steadiness, and then the spreading silence of the gun's bark, and then the silence of the bird not flying away. . . . (119, Buckler's ellipses)

As full as this passage might seem, it is the more remarkable because it follows seven paragraphs luxuriating in the varieties of yellow light on that single October day of "after ripeness." This paragraph lists thirteen types of silence and uses the word "silence" itself six times. The silence is intensified by the many sibilants, particularly by the concentration of s's at the beginning and end. Structurally the paragraph builds from visual images of silence to images of smell and then, as the sensory appeals become more immediate, to the tactile sensations of cool gun-barrel and suspended breath. This movement is neatly capped by the startling paradox of the gun's loud sound being silent, and by the ultimate silence of death. The movement of the paragraph from the carefree flights of birds to the hints of decay to the steady perfection of no breath and the peace of death is a vivid reflection of the movement of the entire novel. Strengthening the effect of the passage is Buckler's verbal ingenuity. He describes the silence of the bluejay's flight as "feeding," an unlikely participle that conveys not only the sense of a nourishing and gratifying silence but also the sense, slightly more menacing, of a silence that consumes, that must be fed. Similarly a sky which is "deepening" is not only becoming darker, but is also, rather ominously, extending itself beyond limits. And, by the simple device of showing the singular "leaf" under the hunter's foot, Buckler startles us with the sound of frozen motion. On the one hand, the accumulation of miniscule differentiations implies, paradoxically, a pre-linguistic perception—a booming confusion. On the other hand, the occasional deviant usages signal a child's dialect.

Buckler's unusual juxtapositions (other examples in this passage are "memory-smell" and "camphor-breath") add a strangeness to the trancelike effect of the list itself. Magic is as important as meaning. After the first sentence no predicates move in the paragraph; although the silence clearly has its own internal dynamism, action, like breath, is suspended. Not surprisingly then, the passage makes in itself no narrative sense and has little connection to the narrative of the novel: we don't know which hunter, or what bird, or what happened to the deer which seemed to be the hunter's original quarry. Buckler added his favourite punctuation, the ellipsis, when he revised this passage to emphasize a recurring, uncompleted "and then . . . ."[8] There is so much said, yet so much left to be said, that the reader is left slightly mesmerized.

Although this paragraph is not explicitly defined as David's point of view, it is worth remembering that we first meet David "in a kind of spell" (14), staring distractedly through the window at the valley and the mountains. The overwhelming plenitude of things often sends him into the kind of trance we would associate with the total absorption of a child's game. Indeed his own lists, and the clamour within his own brain, are so prominent in such passages as the catalogue of silences that it is difficult to make a complete separation between the narrator's perspective, so immediate and so much from the inside of community and family, and David's own perception.

The difficulty of making the distinction suggests, of course, that the narrator is telling the story that David yearns to tell in a way David never recognizes is appropriate to it. The suitability of Buckler's style to David as child may also indicate why in *The Cruelest Month*, that very adult book depicting a sort of Bloomsbury in the Annapolis Valley, the overflowing style is so much less effective, seeming to be an affectation rather than a technique closely integrated with content. On the other hand, where it is more neatly balanced with a plain colloquial style, a style based on lists or catalogues is mostly effective in *Ox Bells and Fireflies*, a fictional memoir which begins and ends in childhood.

Behind every list lies Buckler's passion for exactness, not a pared down exactness, of course, but a full and encompassing exactness. Buckler's attitude seems to be that if one verb, or modifier, or simile, will not reach a particular reader, then another will. This attitude is implicit in the memorable—to some, infamous—sentence marking the breathless anticipation of Christmas Eve: "In that instant suddenly, ecstatically, burstingly, buoyantly, enclosingly, sharply, safely, stingingly, watchfully, batedly, mountingly, softly, ever so softly, it was Christmas Eve" (65). This sentence contains an adverbial phrase, and fifteen adverbs. It's the sort of sentence which would have moved D.H. Lawrence to shout "Ernest, leave off." But the excess is the very thing which makes the sentence worth examining.

Dream, in the exaggerated spirit of David's "I-will-be-the-greatest-in-the-world," drifts through this passage, but accompanied by a kind of economy too. Because the core of the sentence is the vague pronoun "it" and the bland verb "was" each adverb introduces its own possible agents and actions. "Suddenly," for example, describes the surprising way the time arrives, but "watchfully" suggests a prior time with a boy vigilantly waiting, while "softly" describes a sound and the responsiveness of one person to another. The sequence of adverbs shows some striking similarities to the list of silences, driving early to a climax of abrupt force in "burstingly," then floating unevenly through both "softly" and "stingingly," to the familiar sense of suspended breath, and an end in gentle silence. The child visionary is never more obvious; David could not string together fifteen adverbs—he is in a trance, almost made explicit by "ecstatically," but deepened by the rush of paradoxes and shifts of subject. The sentence seems almost reckless, and yet there is that sense of rightness again. If we try to remake the basic sentence, placing the adverb next to the verb—"it was softly Christmas Eve"—we recognize that for Buckler passion triumphs over syntax. The drafts of the novel in the Ernest Buckler Collection at the University of Toronto Library reveal that the pattern was carefully calculated. At one point the key adverbs "batedly" and "mountingly" were placed near the beginning of the sequence, then restored to their present position.

The incremental style is particularly appropriate to David's Christmas Eve because it conveys the stretching out of an experience, and the clinging to a sensation, typical of children. The psychologists' term "centrated," describing the child's overestimation of the size and significance of a thing or event, suggests the peculiar suitability of Buckler's style to *The Mountain and the Valley*.[9] Certainly the hypnotic magic of the lists seems to belong mainly to David, or to the narrator, who is often indistinguishable from David. And the centrated quality of the lists governs the style, from a two-page catalogue of the effects of light to a trio of adjectives, from a list of similes to the selection of a particular metaphor. Like the cubist's overlapping "takes," David's style shows only traces of what a linguist calls child language (or drawing), but it continually implies a child's understanding.

Consider, for example, the multiple interconnections implied by Buckler's similes. The prevalence of simile, that somewhat unfashionable literary device, gives another element of quaintness to a very modern novel. Connecting two elements through *like* and *as* seems, as it were, to keep the soil close at hand, to prevent the fancy's having completely free rein. I suspect that Buckler loves simile because he recognizes that simile makes metaphor more colloquial, and more accessible. A typically ingenious figure of speech shows the need: "The sky was so purely blue from morning till night it had a kind of ringing, like the heat-hum of the locusts" (101). If this sentence is to suggest David's perception then the simile seems the more congenial poetic device for the fourteen-year-old, since it provides some bridge between things as disparate as blue sky and the sound of locusts; it gives a sense of a boy trying to link things together. Buckler's repeated inclination to simile indicates "subjective viewpoint": in *The Mountain and the Valley* the "false absoluteness" of simile conveys the particular view of a man trapped in a boy's dream of exactness. Quite appropriately, then, a touch of the absurd often inheres in the sense of "total identicality" registered by the simile.[10] On the other hand, if "everything seemed to be an aspect of something else" (287), as it does for both David and Buckler, then simile conveys the ordinariness of that experience in a way that metaphor cannot.

In order to see in everything an aspect of something else Buckler is willing to take great risks: "The wind plucked up waves of milk from the pail, like fans of cow urine" (73). The mind of a young boy might well leap to the comparison in appearance, but by using the adult, in this context somewhat euphemistic, "urine" Buckler takes the chance of implying other comparisons that might sink the idyll into bathos. Repeatedly Buckler will take the opportunity to push a simile to its limits: "The North Mountain rose sharply beyond the river. It was solid blue in the afternoon light of December that was pale and sharp as starlight, except for the milky ways of choppings where traces of the first snow never quite disappeared" (13). The first typescript draft of the novel, in the Ernest Buckler Collection, shows that this sentence was once straightforward description: "The North Mountain rose sharply beyond the river. It was solid blue in the sharp December light, with white patches of clearing here and there where the first snow lasted all winter."[11] As the sentence is revised and more figurative language is introduced, the catalogue of infinite correspondences begins to govern the sentence and completely change its effect. Buckler nicely conveys the hint of approaching evening, the touch of the cosmic with its diminishing of man and mountain, and a sense of magic, especially because "starlight" is a light which emanates rather than illuminates. Then, as Buckler draws out the simile into epic proportions, the fantastic takes over completely. "Starlight" describes the quality of light, yet "milky ways," which should be the source of exactly this sort of light, no longer describes the afternoon light but interruptions in the solid blue colour of the mountain. Hence the mountain itself seems turned into a sky, which would, presumably, be generating its own light. Either Buckler has completely lost control of his language, or he is reaching for an impression of floating in an infinite sky, through space. Again his style carries us from immediate contact with the rural world into a dreamlike trance beyond the claims of even poetic logic.

The same mesmerizing plenitude is found in Buckler's metaphors, even in almost incidental passages:

> And now, working in the fields, the obbligato of ache in his head chimed with the quiet feeding orbits of his thoughts (each one branching immediately, then the branch branching, until he was totally encased in their comfortable delta). It isolated and crystallized him into a kind of absolute self-sufficiency. (228)

This paragraph describes an older David, five years after his father's death, suffering continuing pain from his fall in the barn. The metaphors repeatedly jolt the reader out of one frame of reference into another. Thus, while the musical term "obbligato" may suitably lead to the suggestion of bells "chiming," there is no preparation for an abrupt switch to the planetary implications of "orbits," nor for the animation of these orbits in "feeding." Then Buckler uses, albeit parenthetically, a plant metaphor to describe David's thoughts, shifting in the same breath to the river metaphor and the surprising "delta." Yet while the associations of "plain" and "depositing" seem entirely appropriate here, we may be at a loss to explain why David should be *"encased"* in a "delta." Buckler asks his reader to follow him into a new sense of enclosing, before his other, decidely unenclosing, metaphor has run its course. In this context that tired metaphor, "crystallized," takes on renewed vigour, since it is so completely different from the musical metaphor at the beginning of the paragraph.

A writer attempting a closer analogy to actual child language might use the reiterated conjunction "and" (the first acquired by the child), whereas Buckler suggests the same inability to discriminate cause and effect through proliferating random metaphor, more that is, through literary device than through grammar. The passage is the more amazing because it describes pain and loneliness, even if these are seen in a positive light. Buckler is as likely to play his ingenious metaphorical games in gloom as in happiness. Again, the precise feelings seem less important than the literary bravado. I find a lightness in the passage, a freeing from physical realities (such as the pain), into an illusion created by clever prose. Insofar as we are within David's perception here (and again it is difficult to distinguish David from the narrator), we sense that David is protected by his own secret, yet liberating imagination.

One message conveyed by the style is clear: David is happiest when thought is suspended, when thoughts themselves combine and interrelate until everything is fused in a visionary trance. In spite of the new element of physical pain I see a strong similarity between David's crystal isolation in the field and his fishing, while still a young boy, at the beginning of the novel. David has always had the ability to "let his mind not—think" (28)—the phrase is a perfect compact descriptor of the novel's child language—and he cultivates the ability to free himself from language and thought into a mesmerizing sensory apprehension of nature. David's first reaction to the deaths of Spurge Gorman and Pete Delahunt is to escape into imaginings (41); in a sense his reaction to the imminence of his own death is no different. He still dreams of being the "greatest." He still has no perspective: the day he spends fishing on the mountain with Joseph and Chris is "the best time he'd ever had" (29); years later the day he and Toby went to town for the beer "was the best day of all" (257). The experience is made superlative because "there hadn't been any *thinking* about it" (259). Buckler's massed similes and metaphors move the mind in so many directions at once that the reader is left, as in the paragraph on silences, almost entranced. Many of the prominent images in the novel work to reinforce this sensation. The best-known passage on style in the novel, prompted by David's reading of E.M. Forster, suggests the imagery most suitable to Buckler's intent:

> At first he hadn't liked the books. They had more to do with the shadow of thought and feeling which actions cast than with the actions themselves. They seemed blurry. Reading them was like study. But now he found them more rapturously adventurous than any odyssey of action. (244)

Images should make an idea or an abstraction more precise and concrete, but, paradoxically, Buckler's images are often of the most "ephemeral" (232) kind. "Shadow," the solitary image in this passage, aside from the books being described, is a very common image in the novel. Insubstantial and transitory things are the staple of much of Buckler's imagery: shadows, breeze, breath, smoke, light, cloud, fog, mist, snow, and the colours of grey, white and twilight. Perhaps Anna's thoughts about breathing—"It went on steadily, keeping you alive, but you weren't conscious of it at all" (266)—might also serve as a description of Buckler's images: they are usually intangible, yet obviously essential and vital, and they carry with them the idea of suspended consciousness.

When more hard-edged images are used they are often run together in celebration of a perfect, if irrational, unity: "the lemon-green murmurous-needled pine overturned by the wind, its ragged anchor of roots and earth like the shape of the thunder of its own falling . . ." (286). Again, it seems less necessary to follow through the sequence of meanings than to immerse oneself in the cornucopia of sensations: from taste to sight to sound to touch in the first four images, then back to sight and feel and touch until the passage explodes in sound and motion. Again, such nonce forms as "lemon-green" mark a child's not yet separating concepts as discrete words demand. According to M.D. Vernon, in *The Psychology of Perception*, "in young children there is little differentiation of primary sensations from one another, and . . . visual, auditory and other modes of sensation which occur at the same time become so closely linked that in later life perception of one type of stimulus is liable to arouse imagery of the others."[12] Buckler's intuitive psychology constantly reinforces, and then extends, the theory. Because it implies a secondary sensation—a sense of blue produced by a sound rather than a blue dress—synaesthesia sustains something remote, shadowy, in David's contact with the world. Simultaneously, Buckler's synaethesia continues the same accumulation, and surprise, and jamming together, as we find in the larger features of his style. Given the interrelatedness of all things, the "stillness was loud and moist-smelling and clean" (268), and "shape and colour reached out to him like voices" (286).

Similarly, the hyphenated compounds upon which Buckler often depends insist, in themselves, that unrelated things are really inseparable. Buckler fuses two or more things or ideas or sensations, and the resulting concept both contains the separate things and yet becomes a unity which is more than and different from each separate thing. An adolescent eagerness runs together ideas and emotions: the form carries one beyond the physical. Although there are examples on almost every page, I need only mention Buckler's best-known compound, used three times in rapid sequence when Toby leaves for war and his death; "that maybe-the-last-time brightness rushing along with them in the trains" (276). This feeling, curiously, has its closest ties with the 'certainly-the-first-time-brightness' of childhood. The resonant compound sticks with the reader, trembling just beneath the final autumn scene, when the leaves achieve their very brightest colours just before they die and fall.

Seeing the trains go by, sensing that "maybe-the-last-time brightness," David is always a watcher rather than a doer; he learns through words rather than through touch. He contrasts his life with Chris's: "The things that happened to himself were pale, and narrative only. He stayed the same" (199). True, in the sense that David's life seems like something read about rather than something lived. But misleading if we take narrative to imply event, or story, or physical action. Of these, David's life shows relatively little; even in that most physically influential event of David's life, his fall from the barn's rafter, the emphasis is more on motive and response than on the action itself. And of course, Buckler's, too, is a style of watching. He lingers over the tiniest detail and savours its expression in a style which interrupts and delays and almost obliterates sequence. Cause and effect, sustaining of metaphor, unmistakeable meaning are less important than a feeling of absorption, trust, submission. Buckler's style is inwardlooking, private, and in large part, like that of all fine literature, a reality unto itself. David even goes a step beyond Buckler's inwardness, for he is so private that he is terrified of an audience. When Toby reads a sentence of his war story, David throws the whole thing into the fire. Perhaps he is distressed, too, by the contradiction between the relatively spare, colloquial style of his story and his fronding, million-capillaried vision.[13] But certainly he shows again that he has not grown up: he is no more mature about his imagination and its products than he was when he kissed Effie during the school play.

"The world of the adult," observes William Empson, "made it hard to be an artist."[14] So David discovers, and responds by remaining a child. The childishness remains, in the most essential sense, despite the many explicit comments in the novel on the stages of David's growing up. "The essence of childhood," the narrator intones after the shock of David's intercourse with Bess, "is that the past is never thought of as something that might have been different. He was never, even for a moment, all child again" (152). Yet it seems, for example, that David's sexual life ends, after three devastating experiences, at this level of stumbling adolescent experiment. Artistically, and emotionally perhaps, he is still at the end of the novel the sensitive but overwhelmed child, rather than the discriminating mature adult. "The inside was nothing but one great white naked eye of self-consciousness, with only its own looking to look at" (281). This is not the eye, surely, on the verge of a finished achievement, but at the beginning of an adolescent artistic consciousness. As Warren Tallman sees it, David "must create his own knowledge in the image of his arrested, his childish and childlike psychic life."[15] The epilogue, then, while it clearly does not convey a wholly negative attitude toward David, does take a profoundly ironic view of where David is.[16] He achieves an ecstatic peace, to be sure, but it is deeply coloured by his self-indulgent and fruitless dreaming.

As he finally climbs the mountain David's mind swarms with images and memories, and faces and voices:

"Stop!" he cried. Aloud.
But the voices didn't stop.
They added a new voice to their frenzied forking, to the bright singing stinging scream of clarity in the accusation of the unattended. Exactly how did the voice *itself* fluctuate, according to the exact inexactness of the listener's listening? (297)

Unlike earlier moments of exultant trance, this passage describes not sensations but metaphysical puzzles. In this sense, of course, it marks the extent to which David is different from the eleven-year-old in Part One. Yet it follows the most intense and massive inventory of sensations in the entire novel. Perhaps because Buckler is dealing here with abstractions the basic ingredients of his style of accumulation become more evident. Before the "infinite permutations of the possible" David cries " 'stop!' " Buckler interrupts the elliptical multiplication of his prose with four simple, staccato sentences. But then the "infinite divisibility" (292) takes hold again, aurally in the alliteration and assonance, syntactically in the tripling of adjectives, and verbally in the repetition of the root words 'exact' (already used dozens of times in the epilogue) and 'listen.' Even here, then, incantation supersedes meaning as David is enchanted by the spell of multiplication and paradox.

" 'Where *is* that child?' " (301) Ellen asks again when she has finished hooking her rug. In her own doting confusion she has chosen the right word and the right question. David dies in the spell of his childhood dreams—"(The morning of my first trip to the mountain, the Christmas tree, the blindman's buff . . .)"—filled with the same innocent hyperbole: " 'my book won the prize!' " (300). The many colours in David's head all fuse in white, and he is slowly covered by the falling snow.

David's closeness to nature suggests a comparison with W.O. Mitchell's Brian O'Connal which I find so tempting that I sometimes mistakenly write Brian when I mean David. Yet how different they are, especially in this matter of their growing up. Brian learns from the spots of time (marked by his "feeling") that are scattered through his childhood; David retreats into them, and encloses himself in them. Brian will become a dirt doctor, as surely as David will *not* become the greatest writer in the whole world. *Who Has Seen the Wind* spreads out at the end through cycles of time and off toward the horizon; *The Mountain and the Valley* draws together as the last rag is tied into the circle of the rug, and the snow aggregates and unifies. Yet as the last white rag is ironically both pure and blank, the snow both warm and smothering, so the concluding flight of the partridge seems, in its suggestion of awkward ponderousness, to be an ambiguous symbol of visionary transcendence. Buckler himself confirms the depth of his ambiguity by an interpretation of the symbol which is added as the last sentence in the first draft of the novel: "It was like death."[17] Not that this aspect of the partridge's flight diminishes Buckler's achievement. On the contrary, it is one last evidence of the enormous richness of his prose. Buckler's, indeed, are " 'Nude Descending a Staircase' patterns." Duchamp's painting is the perfect image for his style: draftsmanlike precision expressing, paradoxically, the impossibility of completely separating out one distinct image, the cinematic magic, the delicate distinctions among essentially monochromatic shades, the multiple overlapping images at once static and spatial yet containing the movement of time. Recall that David wonders about "a man who would *draw* like that" (296). He thinks of Duchamp not as a painter, but as someone who, more childishly, simply draws. Some connection seems to exist between the child's early use of synchronic vertical constructions in language and the associated images in Duchamp. Indeed Maurice Merleau-Ponty claims that the child has an instinctive empathy for cubism before he learns the culturally dominant way of representing the world:

It is altogether startling to see certain children much more apt to understand this drawing or that painting by Picasso than the adults around them. The adult hesitates before this kind of drawing because his cultural formation has trained him to take as canonical the perspective inherited from the Italian Renaissance.[18]

Nor is the allusion to Duchamp out of place when we consider David as artist. Marcel Duchamp is distinctive among modern painters because he produced only a very few paintings; he is the "personification," writes William Rubin, "of Dada's refusal to distinguish between art and life."[19] Instead of developing experimentally through many hundreds of works, Duchamp created but one painting marking each stage of his development. Rubin, in pondering this curious artistic career, gives a fascinating hint of the kinship between Duchamp and David: "Duchamp advances speculatively, not by painting but *by cerebration*."[20] And, to note just two other connections, both the sexual content of the painting and the irony of its implicit mechanization may have more bearing on where David is than first appears.

One especially illuminating reaction to "Nude Descending a Staircase" is X.J. Kennedy's intense lyric of the same title:

Toe upon toe, a snowing flesh,
A gold of lemon, root and rind,
She sifts in sunlight down the stairs
With nothing on. Nor on her mind.[21]

Here, too, are hints as to why David should single out this particular painting: because of its suggestion of a frustrating innocence, and because of its expression of the harmony of no-thought (though David, presumably unlike the nude, arrives at this state through intense, clamorous thinking). Buckler's prose, perhaps paralleling the poem's style, though much more profusely, multiplies images rapidly, echoes and re-echoes its rhythms and sounds, and joins all the senses, to become a marvellous maze. Like Duchamp's painting, Buckler's novel is an ironic comment on naïveté, and a luminous celebration of delight without judgement.

6

Emily Carr and the Language of Small

In one of the languages there are no nouns, only verbs held for a longer moment.

Margaret Atwood, SURFACING

"Small was wholly a Cow Yard child."[1] In this seven-word paragraph which seems all the more abrupt and simple after the luxuriating plenitude associated with David Canaan, Emily Carr introduces the persona who incorporates her memories of childhood. Versions of Small shape most of Carr's writings: in *Pause*, "the fat girl," alien and innocent, is the animateur; Carr's Indian name, Klee Wyck, the Laughing One, honours the uninhibited openness of childhood; even in *The House of All Sorts* Carr, as landlady, continually presents herself as utterly naive. Mary Louise Craven concludes, rather sternly, that "the persona that emerges most clearly [in all Carr's writing] is that of the 'smacked child'—maligned, misunderstood and 'hurt.' Carr's response to this 'hurt' is consistent; she retreats from humans to the other worlds of her animals and nature."[2] But *The Book of Small* is mostly Cow Yard and little hurt; Small sees afresh a vibrating world.

To turn from the precise character of Carr's persona to consider the language Carr uses to articulate Small's perception is to recognize this emphasis. Carr is a sufficiently shrewd writer—although her talent is seldom acknowledged in studies of Canadian writing—to develop a language for Small, not by facile scraps of baby talk, but by attuning herself to a few underlying features and structures of child language. An illusion of simplicity is hard-won: "I've put all I know into it ["The Cow Yard"], lived the whole thing over, been a kid again in the old cow yard." Yet, she insists, "it was never intended for a children's story."[3] Carr overcomes the technical problem of recovering the "kid's" experience without losing the adult reader; Small is young and innocent but she attracts the reader who respects that form of rebellion which is simple refusal to acknowledge the inevitability of defeat.

The form Carr finds suitable for Small is difficult to label. Fictional memoir is the most suitable tag available, yet it describes neither the structure nor point of view of *The Book of Small*. The "fictional," however, appropriately implies that Carr's use of a third-person persona, shows dissatisfaction with the potential superficiality of a memoir in which the writer records strictly what is remembered in her own past. But, as if she senses that novel equals *Bildungsroman*, she avoids the form that structures a progression from adolescence to maturity. A story of childhood, *prima facie* unfinished, where the subject's attention span is shorter, where diverse experiences have equal significance, demands an alternate, more segmented form. As we have seen, Alice Munro's *Lives of Girls and Women*, Margaret Laurence's *A Bird in the House*, and Clark Blaise's *North American Education* all respond to this dictate. (Gabrielle Roy's *La route d'Altamont* is the most obvious French-Canadian parallel.) Yet all of these involve some element of "growing up," a theme Carr seems to resist. The more fragmentary, and less formally consistent memoirs, like Wallace Stegner's *Wolf Willow* or Ernest Buckler's *Ox Bells and Fireflies*, seem closer to the spirit of Carr's. Carr develops a memoir, in the third person and past tense, in which the experiences she remembers, and shapes, appear to the reader as the spontaneous encounters of a child. For example, she uses several variations of "*free indirect style*," where the "thought or speech is only partly rephrased to fit the past tense of the narration."[4] She animates an incident, or a character, as its essentials might hold in the child's memory. A passing reference to Indian memories in Klee Wyck hints at her approach: memories have a life of their own, immanent in place, and they live not in elaborate retelling but in the "brightening" of the eyes, or a few "quick hushed words."[5] Unlike memories in Proust, which the narrator recognizes as part of memory and of the definition of a present personality, the writer's knowing about the memory (which must of course be there in some way) seems, in Carr's fictional strategy, to be deliberately hidden.

The extremely limited sense of continuum between working writer and child character is consistent with Carr's respect for the unique properties of the child's vision. On one of the few occasions when she talked and wrote about her own painting, she turned quickly to the child to illustrate: "The child's mind goes all round his idea. He may show both sides of his house at once. He feels the house as a whole, why shouldn't he show it? By and by he goes to school and they train all the feeling out of him."[6] Carr's Small is a way of showing the insights potential in this combination of intelligent feeling and encompassing perception.

To describe the language by which Carr credibly sustains this point of view—what students of child art call *réalisme logique*—and the discoveries that it makes possible, we might begin by returning to the opening quotation and some more particular comment on the linguistic implications of Small's name. The name itself comes as a surprise, despite the title, because the first section of *The Book of Small* uses proper names, and rarely, the first-person "I."[7] Furthermore Carr gives us no indication where the names—Bigger, Middle, Small—originate, nor to whom they apply. By avoiding any explanation for what is to be a sustained use of these peculiar names she gives validity to Small's perspective: that is, the child would not remember, and would not care, where the name originated. "Small" is an adjective; to use it here as a noun, and a name, is on one level to suggest the child's rudimentary grasp of grammar. More significantly, Carr takes a quality with some emotional content and makes it into something concrete and alive. Appropriately "big" and "little" (small), referring to size in any spatial dimension, are the first spatial adjectives the child learns.[8] Also, these nicknames—and other names such as Bong, or the names for the nurses in *Pause*—suggest community jargon, as if these are private names giving affectionate definition to a particular closed family. Yet the connotations of intimacy are rather slight. Instead, austere naming through impersonal abstractions, especially in references to "the Father," is more noticeable. But the perspective of the child is undoubted: she apprehends some elements of dimension and comparison, is a loner, and she is still egocentric, perhaps not yet recognizing the others in her family as individual personalities.

Yet *The Book of Small* is not self-reflexive in any very obvious way. Indeed, as I have said of the name Small, the impressive feature of Carr's style is its unselfconscious use of child language. The child Small shows no obvious interest in the texture of words, in language as language, and very little in books or story. This attribute is, of course, consistent with the child's general lack of metalinguistic awareness.[9] The reader's pleasure is similar to the delight a parent finds in the unique usages and spontaneous discoveries of the young child's language. For me the delights of Carr's particular child language rest in three areas especially: an idiosyncratic diction, the prominence of concrete finite verbs, and a syntax and organization emphasizing presentness of perception. From the beginning I should insist that these features appear overtly only intermittently but often enough to remind us of the child modality.

The idiosyncratic diction, particularly the frequent coinage of words unfamiliar to the adult vocabulary, stands out. In the opening sketch, for example, we find the noun "make-believes," the verb "taggling," or the adjective "Englishy" (8-9). Often, elsewhere, in commenting on her writing, Carr insists on the merits of the untutored: "they'd [my manuscripts] do their job better, I feel, in my own words than in A-1 language that does not belong to me."[10] Her "own words" are obviously not all from the early stages of language learning, but she sprinkles her writing with eccentric usages—her father "was always very frowny"; a story is "as fairy as anything" (13)—as if to signal the perception at hand: that is, the "narrator," speaking of Small in the third person, uses Small's language and presents her not in mature reflection, but as Small would perceive herself.

Although the surprising "splank" of a rose blossom in *Hundreds and Thousands*, or the mysterious "cobwebby" darkness in *The House of All Sorts*, reveal Carr's general preference for an unpolished vocabulary, the child neologisms are particularly prominent in *The Book of Small*. In *Klee Wyck*, a work with which it otherwise shares linguistic features, there are, for example, almost no obvious coinages. By far the largest number of Carr's idiosyncratic word choices are adjectives, most often formed by adding -y, or a variant, to nouns, or less frequently, to verbs: on Sunday her father "was very *camphory*"; the trees on the lamp posts at Christmas are "not *corpsy* old trees but fresh cut firs" (4; 119; my italics). Such formations authenticate the child's perspective by showing the extension of a grammatical rule: Small, sensing that some adjectives are formed from nouns by adding -y (e.g., flower-flowery), applies the rule broadly as she develops her own language.

On the semantic level there are several significances. The -y suffix is a diminutive, making the world fit Small's dimensions: a "corpsy" tree is smaller than a "corpse-like" tree. More importantly, Carr creates a sense of a quality completely suffusing the thing or person described, and inseparable from it. "Father smelled strongly of camphor"—with the same deep structure—would suggest a mind much more able to discriminate and place things, or experiences, in categories. Small's father, at this point, is totally identified with camphor. On the other hand, the adjective implies a judgement not found in the use of a noun as "stater"; the irregular formations at first suggest naïveté which veils but does not entirely hide the writer's opinion.

One of the most striking coinages, perhaps because it is the first to appear in the book, is an adverb describing the Saturday night bath. Carr exclaims, "If you wriggled, the flat of the long-handled tin dipper came down spankety on your skin" (3). Here the buried verb "spank" lends both sound and greater action to the scene. Indeed, despite the prominence of such coined adjectives as "nobbledy roots" and "boggy ooze" (146-147) actions, not states, are central to Carr's language in *The Book of Small,* and throughout her work. Idiosyncratic diction is frequently noticeable in Small's formation of a noun from a verb, as when the Cow's sniffs among the spring willows are described parenthetically as "all puff-out and no pull-in" (18). The strategy of containing an action in the form of a noun suggests passivity, but gives tactility to an otherwise vaguely sensed sound image. The device reflects the child's inclination to learn through touching, to identify her world by turning it over in her hands, to feel her house as a whole.

But the feel of action vibrates more obviously, of course, in Carr's remarkably rich verbs. Writing of the lobby of "Victoria's top grandness," the Driard Hotel, Small/Carr claims: "All its red softness sopped up and hugged noises and smells" (163). Carr's verbs do not show the obvious idiosyncratic formations of her adjectives, but the tactility,the metaphorical dimensions, and the occasional ungrammatical usages of her verbs link them to the emerging language of Small. Certainly Carr asks that her verbs do more than convey an action. If Carr does not use more verbs than the average writer, their oddities, in combination with the other aspects of her grammar, at least make us think of her as verb-oriented, as if her verbs are "held for a longer moment." One of the characteristics of child language is its high proportion of verbs; in emphasis, if not in numbers, the language of Small mimics this feature.[11] Carr on Small, like a child, talks a great deal about action, about "what happened to what and who does what."[12]

In this world of happening and doing, Carr's verbs animate the inanimate and anthropomorphize the non-human. In the Driard lobby, the abstraction "softness" becomes, by virtue of two unpredictable verbs, active and human. Like "the growth-force springing up so terrifically" in Carr's rain forest, and in her later paintings, everything in Small's Victoria is bursting with growth.[13] The pervasive animation is likely to remind us of the most memorable feature of Dickens's brilliant child language which makes even the most somberly static room—Mr. Dombey's library, for instance—move and breathe. For Carr, as for Dickens, settings have an extremely powerful influence on the observing child. At one moment a "wonder tickled your thinking" (65); at another the "sky spaces . . . lapped up" the gulls' cries (81); at yet another, "the wind sauntered up the stream bumping into everything" (71). Carr's metaphors are almost always contained in verbs. One has to search diligently in *The Book of Small* for conventional metaphors of the "x is y" pattern; similes are much more noticeable. The accumulation of so-called "active metaphors"—and these are just a few random examples—creates two complementary effects essential to Small's way of showing the world to herself: as a place where animals are more lovable than humans, and where touching reveals all sides of an object at once.[14] In one of the few overt statements of norms in the book, Carr tells us, "I loved Mrs. Mitchell because she loved creatures" (134). Carr's humanizing of animals and animating of the inanimate constantly reinforces this moral criterion. If, in Carr's world, the human ties are limited, she has an active, a "felt" contact with all of the non-human: the verbs, characteristically rich in imagery, appeal most surely to the sense of touch. Both the sopping up and hugging of the hotel's sofas insist on knowing through physical contact. From Lizzie's "squeez[ing] out of" (8) the Sunday walk round the garden, to Victoria's "pok[ing], bulg[ing] and hollow[ing] over" (126) its eccentric citizens, most of Carr's most vivid active metaphors imply the child's reaching out for physical contact with the world she wishes to name.

As daring as its verbs might be, the suggestions of tactile contact give a sub-text of practicality to *The Book of Small*. Indeed, despite a few, a surprisingly few, flights of fantasy in Small, Carr more often denies the attraction of "fairyland" (11). Small finds sufficient wonder in the physical and animal worlds. Carr's language, then, especially the verbs, implies that Small understands her world as naturally fantastic. She marvels at an orange lily (which she predictably personifies as "Lily"): "The entrance to her trumpet was guarded by a group of rust-powdered stamens—her powerful perfume pushed past these" (56). Such balancing of the intangible ("perfume") with the physically vital ("pushed past") gives to so much of Small's world the natural magic of lightning and morning mists—things not quite animate, yet surely not inanimate.

I have been suggesting that Carr's prose might be read as a poem, that she scrupulously chooses her verbs for their richness of imagistic and semantic implications. Yet such analysis may miss an aspect of these verbs closer to the subject of actual child language. "Sopped up" and "hugged" are certainly extraordinarily vivid, partly because they evoke experiences (spilled milk?) common to the child. They may, on the other hand, at least suggest the child's using a limited vocabulary as a strategy for discovery. "Sopped up," with its incongruous pejorative associations of the sloppy and soiled, may not, that is, be the *mot juste*; at any rate, it is certainly completely different in its associations from "hugged." The unlikely collision may represent a child's overextensions of meaning, just as Carr/Small overextends rules for adjective formation. On the other hand, the simpler explanation is that Carr's metaphors suggest a child making a connection between two domains on the basis of a single, surface similarity without consideration of the (more adult) ingenious multiplying of the metaphors. In either case, throughout Carr's writing, but most notably in *The Book of Small*, we sense the child: she wants to communicate, or to draw the adult's attention, using a word that "best fits," even if she "knows it is not quite right."[15]

On the opening page, for example, Carr writes of the kitchen pump: "It was a sad old pump and always groaned several times before it poured" (3). A normally transitive verb is used intransitively: the subject, in the usual grammatical context, is always the substance being poured, not the vessel from which it is poured. Carr again is animating Small's world; but the variation from standard usage also creates the sense of a young child searching for the correct language. An incompletely developed grammar is certainly obvious in such miscues as "Mr. Scaife, a pioneer, had digged a deep ditch round his forest field" (82). But similar associations may cling to other of Carr's linguistic adventures, such as her making a verb from a noun ("Dr. Reid amened," 6); or a verb from an adjective ("The up ends of all the logs higgledy-piggledied into the sky," 128). Many such alterations build the impression of a Small world, continuously active and bursting with energy and experienced as Small's words would shape it.

As we shall see, Carr also makes a good deal of effort to reflect Small's shaping in the structure of the sections of *The Book of Small*. But the syntax of individual sentences seldom shows the distinctive turn we have noticed in Carr's diction and verbs. Ira Dilworth, Carr's close adviser and literary executor, has described what she called " 'peeling' " a sentence as "a process which involved stripping away all ambiguous or unnecessary words, replacing a vague word by a sharper, clearer one until the sentence emerged clean and precise in its meaning and strong in its impact on the reader."[16] Yet such "peeling" does not, I think, result in a particularly high proportion of simple sentences, probably not as great as in Margaret Laurence, for example. Undoubtedly there are many short sentences, but they are impressive not because they occur together but because they contrast with the more complex surrounding syntax. The sentence-paragraph, "Small was wholly a Cow Yard child," is perhaps the best example. Another is found in the same section:

Lilacs and pink and white may filled the air with sweetness in Spring. Birds nested there. The Cow walked on a wide walk paved with stones when she came to the Pond to drink. (16)

Very short sentences might be a way of featuring the sprightliest verbs, but the most concrete verbs are not in such sentences. The sentence, "Birds nested there.", is arresting, though the reason for the emphasis is not immediately clear. Small seems to detect something momentous, but unstated, in the bird's nesting. On the other hand, since the sentence has a

dubious grammatical connection to what precedes it (where is "there"?),
and elusive thematic connection to the following sentence, it ideally evokes
the child's suddenly shifting attention.

But short simple sentences do not in themselves suggest the child's
mindset. The ungrammatical placement of the clause in the last sentence of
this passage works similarly; its very accidental appearance makes it
persuasive. Just as in her dialogue Carr allows Small an occasional bit of
obvious child grammar—" 'Don't want to go!' " (42)—so do lapses from
standard grammar in the text create a convincing child language, but they
are never frequent enough to make her either tedious or cloying.

A contrast with other of Carr's works, however, will at least suggest that
there is something particularly peeled and direct about the syntax of Small.
Even the companion piece, "A Little Town and a Little Girl," which is
published by Clarke Irwin under the umbrella title, *The Book of Small*,
suggests some of what is left out in "The Book of Small" itself. The latter,
abbreviated version has almost none of the conventional qualifying
phrases— "long before I was born," "years later" (76)—which, along with
the much more prominent first person "I" narrator, often signal the stance
of reflective reminiscence. In "The Book of Small" per se, there is none of
the nod to a wider history and geography which gives a touch of the
travelogue to "A Little Town." To be sure, the dominant modality is still
that of Small, the perspective of someone little, in a world somewhat
miniaturized, but Small/Carr in the earlier work hides most evidence of
remembering and never introduces herself with the essayistic note, "as I first
remember it—."

In the first half of *The Book of Small* we are seldom aware of memory at
work. Perhaps the most striking syntactical indicator of this aspect of the
text is to be found where I began—with Carr's interest in naming. Once Carr
settles on the name Small, in "The Cow Yard," she seems to use it as a child
would of a doll or animal or as a child would use her own name; in other
words, she overuses it, a touch obsessively, as if she hasn't yet mastered
pronouns. The same effect appears in her references to "the Man" at the
end of the same story, in reference to "Father" in the first story, and even to
accounts of "horses" in "Ways of Getting Round" (90-91). Perhaps the
scarcity of pronouns in the speech of mother to child is echoed in Carr's
presentation of Small.[17] At any rate, since pronominalization is the most
usual way of providing cohesion in texts, that is of linking one sentence to
those that precede it, an avoidance of pronouns tends to make a text less
fluent. When a proper name is reused, it's as if the writer is beginning again,
as if the sentence in question can be left to stand unattached, the authentic
perception of the moment. Carr manages to suggest, again by relatively
occasional use of a linguistic feature, that Small's perception might be allied

with the holophrastic, non-combining level of syntactical development. Child syntax, in a layperson's view, seems to lack syntax. And in the larger grammar of Carr's sketches, as in the structure of the book as a whole, this lack of fully developed standard syntax is mirrored, concentrating the sense of the enclosed, self-validating world of Small. The angle of vision is very accurately conveyed by Joseph Church's description of egocentric speech: "It is almost as though the child assumes that he and his listener are surveying a common landscape from a common vantage point and have identical interests and concerns, so that all he has to do is point to a few key features to make himself understood."[18]

Some of the pointing is also done, not by linguistic particulars, but by the structure of individual sketches, and of the book as a whole. Most sections of *The Book of Small*, as in most of Carr's prose, are themselves composed of a series of short sketches, almost self-contained. The account of the Pond Place, two paragraphs near the beginning of "The Cow Yard" (16), is narratively discrete: it could be omitted without its absence being noticeable. The last two paragraphs of "Cook Street" leave the announced subject behind, to end with a description of the odd customs of the Chinese vegetable gardener; there's a feeling of afterthought, of something left unfinished. For all Carr's exquisitely careful attention to ordinary elements of the apprehendable world, this juxtaposing of discrete pieces consistently points to a child surprised, so that a reader might be startled into fresh seeing, as well as to the attention wandering, to a carelessness about an adult's (or narrative's) conventional, sequential expectations.

Carr never gives dates and seldom mentions the ages of Small or her family. She ignores chronology (again I am assuming the published ordering of the pieces is Carr's own), so that Small's parents appear after their death has been reported (38). Conventional narrative is almost non-existent: elements of a story sequence, such as details of Small's long wait for a dog of her own, are almost surprising. Small/Carr often ends, it seems, before she is finished, or uses apparent non sequiturs. The reader suddenly begins reading about a slaughterhouse, in a sketch titled "Saloons and Road-houses" (87), and has to read two and a half paragraphs to put the subject in context.

The holophrastic stage of language development, when the child conveys so much, metonymically, using only one-word sentences, provides a fruitful parallel here. We know that with very "limited linguistic resources" the child is able to communicate effectively by using a "single-word utterance to refer to the aspect which held greatest uncertainty or contained the newest information . . . the utterance is informative *from the child's point of view.*"[19] If Carr is faithful to the child's point of view, she need not take account of the reader's desire for more complete information: for Small, at this point, the slaughterhouse is significant—it is informative to her.

In other words, Carr's use of "Small," where a pronoun is standard, reflects a general, and very effective, stylistic strategy. Just as the introduction of Small is a startling departure from the first person "I" of the opening sketch, so the sudden return to "I" ignores the reader's need for information. In "White Currants" Small talks of "it" for three paragraphs before we find out what she refers to. The absence of pronouns quite strikingly suggests a child speaking; the effect is extended by Carr's rarely presenting an earlier subject as something the reader is familiar with. Although she has already told us about the Reformed Episcopal Church on Humboldt Street, the identification appears as new information thirty pages later: "On the corner of Humboldt and Blanshard stood the Reformed Episcopal Church" (112, 144). There is no acknowledgment of an earlier reference: each thing or event, or person, even, in a sense Small herself, appears with the freshness of something first perceived, something which is the "newest information" to the child's awareness. A description of Yeats's poetry (an unlikely comparison, to be sure) provides an elegant summary of the effect of Carr's absence of back reference, of her reference to things without introduction: "Lack of respect for ordinary principles of topic definition . . . conveys a feeling of internality, a notion that the reader is always overhearing an internal discourse of the poet."[20] The effect of Carr's *Book of Small*, and to a slightly lesser extent, of most of her semi-fictional prose, is of a child's talking, almost to herself, with a tremendous sense of the immediate sensory and emotional experience, with scarcely a hint of past or future. In its insularity Small's world might even be a personal version of Carr's sense of Canada; one should come to know both through their immediate presentness: "I did not long to go over to the Old World to see history, I wanted to see *now* what was out here in our West"(85).

Small has a privileged knowledge, and she speaks/writes as if she is not yet aware that she must share that knowledge explicitly in order to communicate. Although she does not have the benefit of intonation and gesture, the reader is somehow in the position of a parent, having to guess at the context, to fill in, and then to smile at the surprising turns—and unintentional insights—in child language. If we linger, now, over a particular passage at greater length, we will discover a fuller sense of the pleasures inherent in Carr's child language. Here we may appreciate not only a single element of Carr's language in isolation, but something of its cumulation, and something of the several elements working together.

"Singing" is the fifth section of *The Book of Small*. Other than the dominating perception of Small, it has little narrative link with the rest of the book. There are, to be sure, references to familiar characters—to her mother, sisters, especially, to the Bishop—and to a familiar place, the cow-yard. Yet no overt theme ties "singing" to the preceding or following section. Characteristically, three sections or variations compose this short segment (just five pages) of Carr's memoirs: the reaction of family to Small's singing, the reactions of an outsider to Small's description of her singing, and Small's own reaction to the singing of her mother and a friend. Singing, here, is implicitly linked to art—for Small's singing is untutored, spontaneous, free, crude, vital, and a (secret) expression of love. When in the last section of "Singing" we see Small on one of those very rare occasions when she is a part (albeit silent and hidden) of the adult world, the connection is possible, in effect, because the adults have reverted to childhood, tumbling forth with songs they haven't dared sing in years.

The subject, in one way or another, unifies the three segments, yet as "stories" the three are radically different, in length, characters, and significance. As throughout *The Book of Small*, no temporal transition joins the pieces. Adverbs of time, references to clock time or to the sequence of seasons, these are the commonplace devices of narrative tradition which Carr/Small so diligently ignores. At the beginning of the third section we learn that "Small's four sisters and her brother went holidaying to a farm in Metchosin." But whether this incident follows the Bishop's visit by a week or several years, or indeed, if it occurred earlier, we have no way of knowing. Carr does not present the incident as part of a temporal sequence, as an adult's conscious remembering, but rather, presumably as it occupied her in childhood, for its immediacy of sensation and emotion. As a child learns verbs before tense endings, or learns words for actions, possession, location, even non-existence, before words designating time, so Carr's child language shows relatively little concern for temporal syntax.

Other than the thematic connections, the most significant unifying principle in "Singing" lies in metaphor: Small's is a world seen from "there among the creatures" (29), a world viewed from the cow-yard. To the child in the first section the cow up close is all geometric perfection, a study in straight lines. In the second section Small recognizes something cow-like in the Bishop: "His deliberate chewing of the words, with closed eyes, reminded her of the cow chewing her cud" (30). The last section ends with a discovery realized through another extension of the cow metaphor (which, incidentally, is the most obvious poetic device linking the entire book):

> Here were two ladies nearly fifty years old, throwing back their heads to sing love songs, nursery songs, hymns, God Save the Queen, Rule Britannia—songs that spilled over the drawing-room as easily as Small's cow songs spilled over the yard, only Small's songs were new, fresh grass snatched as the cow snatched pasture grass. The ladies' songs were rechews—cudded fodder. (33)

In one way or another, throughout this chapter I have tried to describe the stategies which impart this newness and freshness to Small's songs. In "Singing" we again find the apparent child neologisms ("White"—as a noun, "Mother-ladies," "cowsongs," "rechews"), the strange verbs (the participle "cudded"), and the unusual active metaphors ("twiddled," singing "boiled over," "gold watches hiding,") which involve the reader in the novel experiences the child wants to share. But, by a closer examination of the first paragraph of "Singing" we can also recognize some complementary, and less obvious, features of Carr's language of Small:

> Small's singing was joyful noise more than music; what it lacked in elegance it made up in volume. As fire cannot help giving heat so Small's happiness could not help giving song, in spite of family complaint. They called her singing a "horrible row," and said it shamed them before the neighbours, but Small sang on. She sang in the cow-yard, mostly, not that she went there specially to sing, but she was so happy when she was there among the creatures that the singing did itself. She had but to open her mouth and the noise jumped out. (29)

Carr begins, characteristically, by implicitly raising questions: when did Small begin to sing, and why is it a subject demanding the writer's or reader's attention? The questions are unanswered; questions that would not occur to Small do not occur to Carr as narrator. There are no simple, nor particularly short sentences, in this paragraph: Carr does not "peel" her sentences to Small's level by reducing everything to a subject-verb-object format. Indeed, on the contrary, something archaic, and a hint of syntactic struggle touch this paragraph. The first sentence is balanced on the semicolon and again in the parallelism of each half. The declarative, *it lacked elegance but had great volume*, would have been more ordinary, but presumably less representative of Small's point of view, in part because it lacks the vitality of Small's own making. Carr implies, though the syntax itself might be thought slightly more pompous, that the balance is crucial: Small must give up "elegance" in order to attain strength. Again, one might have expected of a "peeling" writer an opening sentence stressing action, rather than state: *Small always sang joyfully, noisily*. But in Small's view singing has an existence of its own, which must be expressed in this way. The absence of a verb here is, as we shall see, a fine strategy to emphasize the vigour of the concrete verb when it does occur. Carr is very attentive to the most effective placement of her coinages and metaphorically rich verbs.

In the second sentence, and again in the third, the proper noun "Small," is surprisingly repeated in places where the pronoun might have been expected. Although the verbs are somewhat dissipated in effect in the early part of the paragraph, no modal verbs (seems, appears, etc.) or "belief qualifiers" weaken the effect of Small's perceptions of the moment. The second sentence, as the first, uses elaborated phrases rather than direct verbs. An emotional state looms large in Small's consciousness, and takes the position of active subject in the sentence.the paragraph moves, then, from description of a state to a state animated (in the second sentence). Or, more correctly, the negative creates a privative form—"happiness" "could not help" being active and "giving song." In this sentence the semantic kernel—Small's almost unconscious singing—is buried; however, the sense conveys potential action, not action realized. The sentence ends with a somewhat misplaced, and therefore abrupt, prepositional adverbial phrase. Again, Carr suppresses the action, using a nominal formed from a verb "in spite of family complaint," rather than saying, for example, *although the family complained.*

The third sentence begins with "they," a pronoun whose reference is rather vague, seemingly to suggest a powerful but rather indeterminate force ranged against her. After a slightly archaic prepositional phrase, "before the neighbours," the sentence ends with a short subordinate clause. In contrast to the dwindling force of the second sentence, the conventional emphasis at the end of the third sentence coincides with the central semantic point. For the first time "singing" emerges as a direct, active verb, in the shortest, simplest clause in the paragraph "but Small sang on." In other words, the potential song of the various elaborated verb phrases now pops out, almost in spite of itself, in a subordinate clause.

The next sentence confirms the action by repeating immediately the active verb, "she sang," which is followed by a convoluted apology, marked by "not that . . . ." Syntactically, this expression prepares for the first unusual verb in the paragraph. The child almost seems here to be dragging out, defensively, her explanation, as if slightly conscious, at least, of neighbours and family: "when she was," for example, could be readily omitted. Indeed, contrast with a recast sentence, such as *She sang in the cow-yard where the singing almost did itself,* suggests how a syntactic delay makes the surprising reflexive verb much more effective. "Singing," which is merely described earlier in the paragraph, suddenly takes on action of its own as something occurring so spontaneously, so without thought, that it has its own vital existence apart from Small.

This change leads to the shortest sentence, at the end of the paragraph, and to the most concrete, active, finite verb. All this I am arguing, is carefully—though not necessarily consciously—prepared to reinforce syntactically the spontaneity of song. In this short sentence we see the strategy of the entire paragraph continued: the archaic inversion in an elaborately compounded verb phrase, "she had but to open her mouth," precedes the direct, simple subject-verb pattern of the second clause. The difference between Carr's expression and the more colloquial *she only had to*, or *as soon as she opened* is striking: an active, colourful verb bursts out of the paragraph, almost in spite of the steady attempts of grammar to curb its vigour. The cumulative effect concentrates in "jumped," despite the past tense, a sense of immediately present action; as throughout, Carr's tactic is to blur any sense of an adult knowingly remembering. The "happiness" that "could not help," and the "singing" that "did itself" are affirmed by the framework of the paragraph in which the abstract qualities of the singing give way to an animate force. "Noise" shows its "joyful[ness]" by "jump[ing] out."

This analysis demonstrates that however proudly Carr wore her ignorance of correct English, the hours of labour she talks of giving to these small prose pieces show in superbly crafted effects, and in a subtle appreciation of the child preception, which may escape the first-time reader carried along by Carr's apparently fluid simplicity. The language of Small, Carr's grammar evoking a self-contained child's world, combines obvious neologisms, insistent foregrounding of verbs, and the sort of shrewd use of syntax I have just noted in "Singing" to represent the child's fresh seeing, not the adult's remembering.

We have surprisingly little serious study of Emily Carr as *verbal* artist; perhaps the best "criticism" of Carr the writer is Florence McNeil's sequence of poems, *Emily*. For McNeil's Emily, writing is no idle diversion: she "wrestle[s] with words" in the "swirl of a sentence." Recalling Carr's own tribute to the child eye in "Fresh Seeing," McNeil imagines Carr's voice as she responds to criticism that her paintings are mere child's drawings:

> these children's pictures
> are deceptive   ladies
> wild colonials   they have
> few rules
> their stark behaviour
> is
> unpredictable.[21]

This primitive simplicity—an art tough and spontaneous, not a sentimental innocence—swirls in Emily Carr's unpredictable and deceptive child's language.

7

Infant Sensibility and Lyric Strategy: P. K. Page, Dorothy Livesay, and Miriam Waddington

It was a pleasure to find out from kids that a bald man had a barefoot head, that a mint candy made a draft in the mouth, that the husband of a grasshopper was a daddyhopper.

This child was drawing flowers; around them she drew several dozen dots:
   "What are those? Flies?"
   "No! They are the fragrance of the flowers."
                     Kornei Chukovsky, FROM TWO TO FIVE

                  a boy
         In the listening
Summertime of the dead whispered the truth of his joy
To the trees and the stones and the fish in the tide.
         And the mystery
            Sang alive
   Still in the water and singingbirds.
                  Dylan Thomas, "Poem in October"

Living alone in a caravan with only her pets for company, sketching and painting outdoors whenever possible, writing in enthusiastic tribute to Whitmanesque spontaneity, Emily Carr is Canada's most Romantic artist. Her dream of the simplified language of Small reminds us how completely the child's sensibility has inspired poetry in the past two centuries. As

eighteenth-century rationalism gave way to Romantic imagination-ism, the
child became the most obvious expression of a pre-rational identification
"with the trees and the stones and the fish in the tide." And in the twentieth
century, students of child development, such as the Russian scholar and
children's poet Kornei Chukovsky in his highly selective diary studies,
recorded evidence of children's predisposition to poetry, of the novel
perceptions inherent in their verbal improvisations.

The great manifesto of the necessity of the child's perception to poetry is,
of course, William Wordsworth's *The Prelude* (1850). This meditative
autobiography incorporates many virtually discrete lyrics, which

> endeavour to display the means
> Whereby this infant sensibility,
> Great birthright of our being, was in me
> Augmented and sustained.
>
> (II, 169-72)

Generally, Wordsworth hoped to sustain the infant sensibility through
simplicity, in "a selection of language really used by men" (*Preface to
Lyrical Ballads* (1800)), and a grammar shaped by emotional honesty and
spontaneity rather than by intellectual wit. The poet rediscovers the infant
sensibility, according to one of the most resonant phrases in the poem, in
"*spots* of time" (XII, 208), and, therefore, especially in place and in nature.
In retrospect we recognize in Wordsworth the first of the ecological poets,
celebrating, like Emily Carr, the interfused interdependence of all living
things.

Connecting the child's sensibility, direct expression of emotion, and
natural imagery, is so inevitable a part of the continuingly romantic modern
sensibility that accumulating examples is gratuitous.[1] I discussed in Chapter
1 something of the connection in Theodore Roethke. Probably the
best-known and most influential twentieth-century example is Dylan
Thomas's "Fern Hill," where the ebullient synaesthesia, and continual
misappropriation of lazy adult idiom (e.g., "all the sun long") are the
prominent features of a compelling child language; the impression of the
carefree child is so strong that one often forgets, or ignores, how profoundly
the poem concerns not only the "green" but the "dying."[2]

A.M. Klein might have had the first light of Thomas's summertime
Genesis in mind when he described the poet as the "nth Adam taking a
green inventory/in a world but scarcely uttered, naming, praising."[3] But the
spontaneous, delighted wonderment of a child's first naming has been
almost invisible in commentaries on Canadian poetry. In this chapter, and in
Chapter 9, I want to focus on some Canadian poets who have paid particular

attention to the languages representing the child's perception. Chapter 9 touches more directly on poetry written *for* children and on one form of radical play with early language. Here the lyrics of P.K. Page, Dorothy Livesay, and Miriam Waddington comprehend the more traditional relationships between infant sensibility and adult imagination which poets have explored.

If the lyric is the literary form most accommodating to spontaneity and overflowing feeling, it might also be the form most congenial to the expression of the child's world. As the examples of Wordsworth and Dylan Thomas remind us, it often has been—at least for the child as subject or inspiration. But in a consideration of child languages, in either of the senses in which I have used the term, the lyric poem is a less obvious source of material. The inherent discipline of the lyric—either in formal patterns of stanza, metre and rhyme, or by sheer brevity—seems to have discouraged most poets from developing a distinctive code for the child's perception or from venturing some mimesis of the child's speech or voice. Roethke's caution against the suite in goo-goo has been particularly heeded in the construction of the lyric, where the slightest slip can destroy the total effect. Persuasive examples of the lyric poem speaking identifiably *as a child*—as evocatively as Brian O'Connal's monologues, for example, or as hauntingly, even, as Pip's naming his mother "Georgiana Wife of the Above"—are exceedingly rare.

The main reason that this book gives more attention to prose fiction than to the other genres is that the length of a novel, or a story, allows for a sense of the *process* of a child's growing up (and child language is, of course, a continually changing structure). The contexts of the child's development, and of her physical, social, and linguistic environments, provide frameworks within which to understand the meanings of child language. James Joyce can goo-goo a bit at the beginning of *A Portrait of the Artist as a Young Man* because the scope of the narrative sets the moocow into perspective.

Yet Wordsworth's most famous line on the infant-adult connection suggests that considerable scope remains for identifying child languages in the lyric. The aphoristic quotability of "The Child is father of the Man" depends clearly on its deviation from the semantic and grammatical norm. Wordsworth represents the insight of the child in a phrasing which evokes the child's own speech: the slightly fumbling inversion becomes a creative tautology that keeps adult innocence alive by sustaining child wisdom.

Wordsworth's memorable line is shaped, then, by the notion I have been exploring throughout this book: that writers' representations of the child-mind are often expressed through what they know, or think they know, of the distinctive ways in which children speak. Of course one line, even if the most familiar, does not go a long way toward defining Wordsworth's child language. More persistent, for example, would be the imagery of transcendent light, the "clouds of glory" which Wordsworth continually associates with the young child. And this feature would be closer to literary convention, and therefore less personal than some hint of the child's actual language. The "tradition of Rousseau and Wordsworth," as W.B. Carnochan explains it, is to recover "the redemptive child in ourselves who in our recollection establishes not only our worth but our identity." The ambivalence of this desire is compactly summarized in "My Heart Leaps Up":

> Though the man may know himself in memories of the child, he may be no less liable to nagging doubts about selfhood, being unable to recollect everything. Wordsworth tries to make self unassailable but cannot quite do it: "And I could wish my days to be/Bound each to each by natural piety." These lines are awkward, the awkwardness reflecting uncertainty.[4]

The intimate language of the child in ourselves is likely to be distanced by, if not lost in the codes of recollection.

The Romantic precedents held out the possibiltiy of a fusion with child language, or, at least, of a discovery through child language of a potential lost in adult expression. The range of realizations of that possibility may be conveniently measured by the distance between the remembering poet and the child recollected. P.K. Page represents the remote observer; in part because she treasures the child's vision before language, the child in her poem is often no more than an implicit *presence* rather than a character in an anecdote recounted. More particular children—a relative, or children playing in a specific place, or on a specific occasion—figure in Dorothy Livesay's poems. In Livesay, that is, the distance closes and the child is *subject*, often nostalgically regarded. Miriam Waddington often tries the still more intimate (and, generally, more difficult) project of having the child as *speaker*, or of blending the child's voice with the poet's so completely that the two are indistinguishable. Examining some of the poetic details along this range from the child as presence in Page to the child's voice in Waddington gives one outline of the child languages in the modern lyric.

In the poetry of P.K. Page, a slightly bizarre, not quite neurotic thoughtfulness shadows the dream of blending child perspective with adult. The child's favourite sculpture, "The Snowman," is analogous to the child's first drawing, but in Page both are multiply empty:

> White double 0, white nothing nothing, this
> the child's first man on a white paper, his

earliest and fistful image is

now three-dimensional. Abstract. Everyman.
Of almost manna, he is still no man
no person, this so personal snowman.[5]

Consistently Page signals the working of the child's mind in such imagery of vacancy and absence. The essence of child language for Page is, paradoxically, the child languageless, and the poet's continual problem is to find words, signs, which lead back to the pre-linguistic:

Who am I, then, that language can so change me? What is personality, identity? And the deeper change, the profounder understanding— partial, at least—of what man is, devoid of words. Where could wordlessness lead? Shocks, insights, astounding and sudden walls. Equally astounding and sudden dematerializations; points of view shifting and vanishing. Attitudes recognized for what they are: attitudes.[6]

In the title poem of her first selected poems, *Cry Ararat!*, Page imagines, by means of the myth of the ark, this puzzle of wordlessness, or of the world disappeared and then rediscovered, unnamed:

Then will each leaf and flower
each bird and animal
become as perfect as
the thing its name evoked
when busy as a child
the world stopped at the Word
and Flowers more real than flowers
grew vivid and immense.[7]

This ideal of a seamless world finally apprehended through the senses, before language intervenes, is at the heart of Romantic mythology and the lyric of lost childhood. For the child, the bird and the word are inseparable: the child cannot separate the concept of the word from the object it signifies. For the adult the ideal exists only in dream, in whose codes—especially birds motifs and "the dream of flying"—Page typically evokes it.[8]

Page's special interest in the child's world is most directly expressed in an uncharacteristically terse poem:

Stefan
aged eleven
looked at the baby and said
When he thinks it must be pure thought
because he hasn't any words yet
and we
proud parents
admiring friends
who had looked at the baby
looked at the baby again[9]

This poem is the most direct, and simplest expression of Page's fascination with the possibility of a way of knowing unmediated by language. Significantly, the adults apprehend the potential by means of a child's speech. The poem organizes itself around a mimesis of child language, rare in Page, as its spareness (also unusual for the poet) embodies the meaning of the unspoken: children, prior to their acquiring language, must have no sense of a separation between self and world. Page's interest in pre-verbal understanding is more typically articulated in the longer, more complicated earlier poem, "Only Child," in which a young boy apparently goes mad, because his mother intrudes words between him and the world of nature:

Birds were his element like air and not
her words for them—making them statues
setting them apart,
nor were they facts and details like a book.[10]

Page's title may suggest that this child is singular and exceptional in his response to the apartness fostered by a language system. Yet the neurotic consequence of language acquisition obviously has broad general implications for a poet who is also a talented visual artist. In the poem an adult observer reports on a mother-son conflict in a studied, almost strained, syntax. But at the end of "Only Child" the poet recreates the dream as it occurred in the boy's mind. As in "Cry Ararat!" Page links the dream, and hence the child's thought, with images of birds and flight. The poet seeking to evoke "the untouched and hardly seen but deeply understood" almost inevitably adopts such a code, pervaded by images which have very indeterminate sensory content. In "Only Child" the repetition of "air," something which cannot be seen, and seldom smelled or felt, is crucial to suggesting a condition of "pure thought"; the image may also remind us of sound, a melody, without semantic content.

This imagery of bird and air is central to Page's idea of the child's consciousness; "Stefan" notwithstanding, she seldom gives a hint of the child's own language because her focus is on the mind before speech. Nonetheless, we might detect in "Only Child" one or two hints of the child-subject's indirect speech—the deviant adjective "slatey" describing the water of the lake, or the possible compound adjective in the phrase "a wet wind feeling." And in this poem the child does eventually speak directly, if in a dream. The last line is a terrifying inversion of the convention of the child's delight in naming the world. The names of the birds chanted— "woodpecker, sparrow, meadowlark, nuthatch"—are no more than a few nonsensical syllables, a sign that the live and loved creatures have been made abstract and lifeless in language.

This theme that contradicts the intricate and revealing patterns of Page's own medium demonstrates the distance I have said exists between P.K. Page and the child. The child is a presence, a vehicle representing a way of seeing, rather than an individual who has been part of the writer's own personal experience. The privileged presence of the child's perception is often evident in the post-Romantic lyric, of course, where no actual child is mentioned: it has something to do, presumably, with the simple apprehension of a red wheelbarrow in William Carlos Williams, as it does, perhaps, with the triple monosyllabic rhymes of Tennyson's "The Eagle." The key elements of the child's presence in Page, however, are those shared by the three Page poems I have mentioned, and poems like these in which the child is not an overt subject: the vocabulary of dream and vacancy.

"Stories of Snow," for example, is in part a demanding metaphysical speculation not explicitly associated with the child's vision. But it is permeated by the imagery of the white or colourless in which Page often expresses the attractiveness of the child's "pure thought" before she has language. This imagery combines with the subject of story, some touches of oral syntax, and a single odd compound in a complex which we might call the signature of the child's presence in Page. The singular phrase which strongly suggests the child's perception near the beginning of the poem is the nonce form "never-nether land,"[11] an expression whose sound, before one considers its punning meanings, signals the child's mis-heard and mispronounced version of a familiar phrase (itself drawn, of course, from a fantasy for children). The same naïve sensibility is reinforced by a syntax associated wth the enthusiastic, but unsophisticated storyteller. "And on the story runs" Page writes in the middle of the poem, reminding us that images and narrative scraps are continually linked by the child's favourite connector "and" (given prominence at the beginnings of lines and sentences).

Page values the child/poet not taking "inventory," but encouraging the world in the state before it is "uttered." The poet, ironically, must express this pre-verbal, "pure thought" in words. In "Stories of Snow" Page's means to a demanding metaphysical speculation lies in imagery conveying the white or colourless, in imagery of dream and of insubstantial nothingness.

The poem is framed by two seven-line stanzas, contrasting a vaguely situated, apparently tropical, or rainforest, land (the richly sensory and constantly growing and changing) with an "area" behind the eyes of pre-linguistic, even pre-sensory perception. In a story in the long middle section of the poem, snow becomes a metaphor for intuitive understanding, a conceit followed every which way in order to suggest the filling up, the inarguable completeness of this world behind the eyes—and, therefore, in the brain, and unexpressed. The story of hunters in a fantastic landscape, with its folk and fairy-tale associations, is an announcement, as well, of the child's presence—as listener, if not as teller.

The "snow-storm [which] sometimes falls/among the lilies" in countries of lush growth must, of course, be "imaginary." Page plays with this irony throughout the poem: white is not only colourless, but it is purely imaginary, the dream of one's pillow as "a northern drift," the "never-nether land" within the glass ornament. In that state come snatches of "story," amounting not to a continuous narrative, but to overlapping complementary images of white: "feather beds" and "flakes," "frozen lakes" and "swans." Everything is suffused with "snow-light falling white," an effect which presumably matches the "breath in plumes," where again something invisible becomes visible. That "plumes" echo both feathers and swans in the same sentence illustrates how cleverly concerted is Page's method, how apparently effortlessly she creates through language that wordless language of total, unlearned, apprehension. Page frequently inclines to imagery which defies sensory definition; the associations in this poem with a child's story and syntax recall, in an odd way, the child's obsessive overgeneralizing I mentioned in Chapter 1. It is as if the poem's speaker has just learned the word "snow" and applies it everywhere: to anything white, to feathers, to breath visible in the frost. The effect is to break down the categorizing hierarchies of language and to reveal the commonality and interpenetration of things.

"Stories of Snow," and its imagery for wordlessness, is far from a representation of actual child language. But among the intimate and multiple connections which have linked child and lyric poem, it is a fascinating example of a poetic strategy for encoding the metaphysics of childhood. Page may not be evidently writing *about* children, but she often aspires to write somehow *through* children. So does Dorothy Livesay; yet her lyrics move closer to particular children: the child is more subject than presence. Her view of the child, from closer up as it were, is less sombre.

Reinhard Kuhn indicates the possibilities of child language for shaping a poetic language to celebrate the world when he notes the appeal of the "naïve relationship between the articulator and the articulated . . . imagined by Rousseau": "voices of children are not instruments of communication, but the very essence of their jubilant nature."[12] Or, as Dorothy Livesay makes the same point: "as a small child I 'felt' words as being linked with music."[13] The child is everywhere in Livesay's poetry, sometimes fragilely "shivering" in such early social poems as "White Fingers,"[14] but, most often, playing joyfully, such as the "boy in the flying field/ . . . pulled to heaven on the keel of a kite" in that important manifesto poem "Without Benefit of Tape."[15] The way the child *sees* particularly fascinates her: "the eye of childhood sees the whole," she claims, while "The inward eye begins as infantile."[16] To present the eye of childhood and the music of play Livesay, unlike Page, uses a language and poetic evoking the naïve relationship between articulator and articulated.

"Perceptions," for example, asserts the precious openness of the child by contrasting the child's unblinking attention to every aspect of the world with the adult's refusal to look. Because the speaker *observes* the child, any "green inventory," either in words or in the child's "draw[ing]," is implied rather than presented.[17] Nonetheless, the caesurae, the abrupt shifts of subject, and the prominence of two-or three-syllable lines, imply the naïve talk of Livesay's own "Small Fry":

> . . . bird brief, irresponsible
> The answer asked
> Not waited for
> And the word punched
> Back like a volleyball.[18]

"Perceptions," in spite of its title, is, like most Livesay poems, more concerned with human relationships (the eye is the revealer of personality, the source of contact between people) than with vision. In a melancholy comment on the adult's deadened senses, and sensitivities, the poem does not indicate what the child is left looking at: it could be the "beauty that only the eye spelled";[19] it might be evidence of human injustice. Ironically, the adult acts like the child, apparently believing that by closing her eyes she can make things disappear.

The "cry" at the end of the poem is crucial, not only because it comes last, but because it combines the lyricism, passion and objectivity that Livesay once insisted were the three necessities for the revitalization of Canadian poetry.[20] Her typical tone melds appeal and celebration; erudition and verbal wit are a minor part of her poetry (compared, say, with Page). Therefore, careful explication of Livesay's poems about children does not necessarily lead us to a sense of a fuller whole. In the opening line, for example, *"shrinking eyes,"* considered grammatically, not only might be what the child sees, but also may describe her eyes. Yet this ambiguity can only be incorporated into the developing meaning of the poem by a too forced ingenuity: that the child is squinting in concentration as he draws. The child's "noting," with its suggestion of a comment, a written observation, seems to contradict the uncritical receptiveness of *"looking."* If we assume that the italicized words in the poem are the child's direct speech, then the language of section one seems spoken in a more sophisticated idiom than that of section three. The middle stanza compounds the difficulties in interpretation. Certainly eyes "snapp[ing] shut" after wide "staring" are completely different from eyes *"shrinking."* Are we to believe that these are descriptions of the same action? Or, as seems more likely, does the shift in tense, and perception, in the middle of the poem, suggest a shift to an adult speaker's view of what happens ("refusing light," in its sophistication, denying the child's view)? If so, the antecedent of "he" cannot be the drawing child at the beginning of the poem.

My questions are not so much an attempt to debunk Livesay's poem as to describe her child language, the way she seems to write through children. What is compelling in this poem is a compact rhythmic embodiment of an emotional truth. The untutored clarity of the child's looking is carried over to the untutored quality of the poem's construction. We might think, for example, of that phase of child language when the child employs pronouns without clear antecedents. Or we might point to more general signs of an affection for the child's perception: in Livesay's "feeling" of words, in her word play, in frequent ripples of a cadence close to nursery rhyme.

But to push the claim for this connection between theme and method leaves me uneasy. At least such an argument needs the context I noted at the beginning of this chapter: post-romantic poetry is almost by definition drawn to the child. More rarely, and therefore more interestingly, the poet will make a conscious effort at the impossible task of finding a rapprochement between an intellectual and metalinguistic understanding of language and the child's use of language (which is, by definition lost to the adult). "The Children's Letters" is Livesay's most successful consideration of this intersection:

> They are my secret food
> consumed in the most hushed corners
> of my room
> when no one's looking
> I hold them up to sunlight
> at the window

to see aright
to hear behind the spindly words
a child's tentative
    first footsteps
a small voice stuttering
at the sky
"bird . . . bird . . ."
Whether these be
my children or my grandchildren
they're ghostly visitors
food of a solitary kind—
they leap on shafts of sunlight
through the mind's
shutters.[21]

The poem pivots on the single word "bird" (that extremely prominent image in poems of child perception), the child's ecstatic repeated cry which the poet imagines she hears. This single instance of the "small voice" enables a new understanding, seems to signal a change in language. That is, in a poem about reading children's letters (both in the sense of something which has arrived in the mail, and the "spindly" forms of the child's handwriting) Livesay recreates the process of discovering an intuitive honesty implicit in child language.

In the poem's second paragraph, the declarative directness of the opening, the confidence in the poet's metaphor, fades. "Bird . . . bird . . . " introduces a conditional clause, an either/or uncertainty, and, most important, a pronoun, "these," without a clear antecedent. What the grammar promises should be a return to conviction proves elusive, both because the visitors are "ghostly" and because the food is vaguely "of a . . . kind" (contrast "solitary food"). Evidently the wise tentativeness of the child, learning to walk and then learning to talk, affects the development of the poem. After the most archaic word in the poem, "aright" (which is also the only strong end-rhyme), the neatness of the poem's language begins to break apart as the child's voice is heard: the left hand margin is abandoned, as silent pauses intrude, and the "t's" and "st's" begin to stutter in the poem's music.

We begin to realize that the process inherent in children making and writing letters begins in the opening of the poem. The persona, retreating to the corner of the room to cherish a secret privately, is mother and grandmother acting as child (also in the *hush*, she is able to devote herself to *hearing* the voices of these children). The initial metaphor might be paraphrased: the child's innocent awakening to the ecstatic naming of language nourishes an inclination in the adult poet to go on discovering language. The apostrophe to the sky, "bird . . . bird . . .," implies a breaking away to freedom. The spontaneous small voice anticipates the most unprepared section of the poem, when a return to the opening analogy to "food" leads to an exuberant shift in metaphor. Instead of the connotations of clarity and judgement associated with the penetrating sunlight of the first stanza, now "they" (the letters? the birds? the children?) "leap on shafts of sunlight." The child's crucial single word, ecstatically repeated, breaks "through the mind's/shutters," to affirm the music and self-reflexive irrational pleasure of the language itself as an embodiment of human freedom.

Like Emily Dickinson, one of her favourite poets, Livesay shows her enthusiasm for children by *describing* their activities, and responding with tributes to their generous trust. Dickinson's characteristic impatient dashes, imperfect rhymes, and syntactical elisions effectively suggest a child's language in many of her poems about children, as do Livesay's easy rhymes, ambient pronouns, and ambiguous modifiers. In Miriam Waddington's poems the distance between observer and subject is not nearly so clear. An instuctive analogy may be found in the poetry of William Blake, particularly the "Songs of Innocence." When W.B. Carnochan summarizes the awkward recollection of self in the child lyric, he makes an exception for Blake: a poem like "Spring," he notes, with its initial absence of person and pronoun, and its later mingling of the imagery of song, bird, and lamb expresses "the poet's ability to dissolve normal boundaries of identity," his "capacity for surrendering his ego to the multiplicity of the world . . . to the experience of childhood."[22]

Similarly, in Miriam Waddington's poetry the poet seems to surrender to child voice and innocence. As in "Fern Hill," the glow of Miriam Waddington's childhood almost dissipates any shadows in her vision. Waddington's spots of time are in north Winnipeg and Gimli:

> The good things of the world
> she learned long ago
> from the sun out there
> in the prairies, in that light.[23]

The nostalgia which typically suffuses the memory of childhood is, in Waddington, at least open-eyed and self-assured; she claims the continuing merit in innocent apprehension. The crucial power of good things learned long ago she sustains in two principal ways: first, again like Dylan Thomas, Waddington, if less boldly synaesthetically, turns constantly to green and gold, frequently combined in the imagery of trees; second (and here Waddington moves away from natural or local spots of time) she uses the narratives of childhood to organize present perceptions. "Portrait: Old Woman," for example, is most vivid and positive when Waddington predicts the woman's elevation to fairy-tale glamour: "you/will be snow-white and/rose-red."[24] In "Snow Stories" Waddington uses an analogy with a child's story to soften an explicit social/political comment:

> This Christmas
> the snow story is
> almost the same;
> we travel and lose
> our way, we fall
> asleep and cannot
> wake up, we are
> under a spell cast
> by the lies of winter.[25]

Indeed, Waddington's commentary is most effective when injustice is viewed rather obliquely, in or against the "good things of the world/she learned long ago."

But, beyond the familiar gardens of green-gold imagery, her development of a short and perhaps stuttering line, and a preference for first-person forms of the verb "to be," more directly mimic a child's voice. But, perhaps, the most compelling use of child language (thought of mimetically) appears in ironic juxtapositions where the child is no part of the overt subject. I think of Waddington falling into a nursery rhyme onomatopoeia in "Artists and Old Chairs," or the single-minded metonymy of her definitions of "Popular Geography": "Miami is one big yellow/pantsuit" and "New York is . . . / . . . the Metropolitan Opera singing/Wagner on winter afternoons."[26] This strategy is at its most audacious when she describes her divorce as if she were a child stumbling with pronouns and verb forms:

> My husband had two wives,
> me and she, but me was legal.
> Signed, sealed, and twice
> delivered, I cookered,
> cleanered, polishered spoons,
> floors, and children.[27]

This combination of innocence and confusion effectively blunts bitterness

and conveys love, but I recognize that many another feminist—for
Waddington is most assuredly a pioneering feminist in Canadian literature—
might read this blundering grammar merely as placing the persona in
stereotyped stupidity. In a study of child language the poem evidently has a
prominence it might not have in a study of feminist poetics: the
overgeneralization of the formation of "delivered" to other verbs marks a
radical shift to a pre-rational understanding, which can be too easily
dismissed as self-trivialization.

Waddington is much less likely than Livesay or Page to draw a sharp
contrast between the child and adult world. The child's language, and
therefore its articulation and understanding of the world, Waddington sees
as continuous—potentially—with the adult's. Showing neither Livesay's
concern to wake up her audience to passion, or Page's intricate verbal
design, Waddington's commitment is to "blazing innocence" and to the
value of the view of the "provincial": both are integral to the child as
expression of active human potential. Her sense of this potential is not so
much argued as embodied: she writes so that the reader cannot distinguish
between child speaking and adult artist remembering. In "Laughter"
(1967),[28] for example, she shows that talent so rare among either poets or
fiction writers, simply to express persuasively the world of the child (but not
by isolating the child; the subject is the plural speaker "we"). The poem
demonstrates how the short two-to-four-syllable line, which Waddington
has cultivated since the mid-1960s, itself suggests something of the child's
limited linguistic constructions (she does not, for example, often use
line-endings to multiply meaning). The poem has no relative clauses and is
entirely in the present tense, both features of child language conveying
spontaneity and the equivalence of varied experiences.

"Laughter" dances through a series of metamorphoses transforming the
speaker (speakers?) into the tiny objects—"dandelion/parachutes," "willow/
catkins," and "curly seashells"—that a child might love—and magnify.
These escapes through daydreaming comprehend air, earth, plants, and sea,
making a liberating laughter possible. Although they are less overt than the
incongruous child formations in "Husbands," suggestions of a child
language in "Laughter" serve to confirm the integrity of the child's world.
The poem is constructed from a series of repetitions in which the
subject—"we"—is never elaborated. The repetition of "laugh" at the end
of the poem also reinforces a child's love of incantation. Where Waddington
uses adjectives, they are the slightly odd tactile coinages the child might
savour—"squirmy," "curly," "knobby."

Waddington's "Laughter" is apparently ecstatic, originating in playful
contemplation rather than in a sense of superiority. But the poem seems
flawed, especially when the last stanza does not resist the inappropriate

ambiguity of a *mocking* "laugh." Indeed, the cost of elements of child language in Waddington is often the loss of semantic layering. For example, the idea of dandelion seeds "tak[ing] the shape" of where they fall, seems to be gained at the expense of the idea that seeds remain seeds to become, yet again, dandelions. On the other hand, if the child is completely absorbed in the analogy of parachutes, the observation may be right enough. And then, as Kornei Chukovsky notes, the younger the child, the more relentlessly simple the repetitions.[29] Certainly in using several poetic strategies suggesting child language, Waddington learns of the indivisibility of adult and child voice, of the fusion of namer and named.

The memory, or idea, of a child's first writing, or first articulating herself orally, mesmerizes most adults when they try to write. The child's first experience with language may have been difficult and puzzling; Robin Skelton describes himself "learning to write/again": his "lines," (presumably both the marks on the page and lines of verse), he realizes "spell"

> not how I hear it
> or say it
> or even think
>
> but in a fashion
> they choose,
> describing a track
>
> through silence,
> in silence,
> answering
> the loud world back.[30]

Or the poet may find the child's discovery in language disconcertingly effortless, as when Dale Zieroth's daughter began

> making noises that sound like questions
> filling in a space around us
> we didn't know was there [31]

Whether easy or difficult, the child's acquisition of language is a key motif in the post-Romantic lyric because it promises a novelty and revelation absent in the poet's usual language, be it the pragmatic language used to buy hamburgers and Kleenex or the poetic sonorities learned in reading Sidney and Keats.

Children's snowmen, children's letters, and children's laughing voices do not define the complete poetic of the child's perception in lyric poetry.

Indeed, if a generalization emerges from my examination of these three poets it is that the lyric poem where it encounters the child sensibly avoids more than a hint of child language, and that something overtly like child language only appears in order to give abrupt redefinition to an adult's linguistically restricted view. Also we recognize that an interest in radical naïveté, and in the language appropriate to expressing its perceptions, should not be mistaken for sentimentality, or lack of craft. Bringing together three Canadian modernists interested in the child and her language does give us one index to the range of approaches to the child in song. In the poetry of P.K. Page the child is a remote but privileged presence, implied especially by a matrix of images of unformed absence. In the lyrics of Dorothy Livesay, the child is an instructive and delightful subject whose presence is conveyed in passionate exclamations, ambiguous syntax, and unattached pronouns. In Miriam Waddington's songs, the child is most likely to appear as singer whose voice is caught in an unambiguous use of words, short lines, or a restricted syntax and repertoire of tenses. In Page's metaphysical arabesques, in Livesay's implicit balladry, and in Waddington's short-line imagism, we have three convincing attempts at that very difficult task—to read and write and sing the language that children speak, and, thus, to incorporate into Canadian poetry some of the intimate excitement of first discovery.

8

A Play Box Full of Plays: James Reaney's *Colours in the Dark*

The one thing we never imitate enough is games, play . . . imitation itself.
James Reaney

Wherever we find a linguistic marketplace, we also find, just outside its gates, and adjacent to each other, a playground and a theater; whenever we exchange words, we also play with them and play—that is, represent*—the exchange of them.*
Barbara Herrnstein Smith

To imitate play and still retain the essential freedom of play is exceedingly difficult. However similar they are, the playground is seldom found in the theatre. The child, and the child's point of view, defies the dramatist, more so than the poet or fiction writer, whose medium is written language alone. Children are offstage, or silent, or adult (as in Arthur Miller's *The Crucible*) or played by adults (as in the musical *You're a Good Man, Charlie Brown*). James Reaney is unusual for so consistently defying the difficulty of imitating play, for so frequently using child characters, and attempting to give dramatic expression to the child's view of the world. Whatever his success—and he seems not entirely to have solved the inherent problems—an admirable bravado wheels through a play like *Colours in the Dark* in which a large cast of children (twelve in the 1967 Stratford production) is active on stage.

Like the poets I have discussed in Chapter 7, Reaney is continually interested in children's letters, and their ability to throw open the mind's shutters. The inspiration of his poetry in the Romantic lyric, particularly in Blake's *Songs of Innocence*, is everywhere evident. His own childhood memories, the potential of the child's imagination, and the objects in a child's world, shape his first lyrics, grow into lyric sequences, and are, in turn, incorporated in many of his plays.[1] In one of his earliest poems, he dreams of "shut[ting] myself up in my play-box hall";[2] in the play *Names and Nicknames* he even includes pre-verbal vocalizations. But *Colours in the Dark*, particularly since in one sense it attempts to understand the childhood orientation of his own poetry, is his most ambitious and comprehensive stage presentation of the child's world. The play is a culmination and pivot in Reaney's own career; moreover, along with George Ryga's *The Ecstasy of Rita Joe*, its impact in Centennial year provoked unprecedented activity, and a new level of artistic achievement, in Canadian English-language theatre.

Colours in the Dark is the play which imitates play in all its manifestations. It is certainly not a play for the critic who insists on a classical dramatic structure, on depth of personality expressed in intense language, or on sustained dramatic conflict. Reaney's play, as he warns in the note to the original production, is a jumble of many plays crammed into one playbox. Again the adult (and learned artist) seeks the re-vision of a child's developing language and perception. But the stage does not allow the leisurely accumulation of Buckler's novel, nor invite, like Page's "Stories of Snow," an attentive re-reading. Reaney the dramatist allies himself with his "hero," variously named and partly autobiographical, who is colouring in the dark; at play in his play Reaney can't keep within the lines, or even tell what colour he is using. All children have this need to scribble, to express themselves in muscle movement made visible. Hence, Reaney's favourite stage of child development: "this is what I want my plays to be wrapped around—the delight of listening to words, the delight in making up patterns (scribbling with your body/bodies) of movement for fun and in play."[3] Such plays, more than most, demand to be read not as books, but as programs for performance.

In the enthusiasm of his scribbling, his patterning, Reaney makes the play an encyclopedia—of colours, flowers, planets, and vocations. *Colours in the Dark* also comprehends a great many kinds of discourse; not only does the slackest of colloquial dialogue join with concentrated lyricism, but the play also contains a child's letter, many hymns, a want ad, a boarding house menu, and county statutes—in short, an encyclopedia of verbal forms. A random clutter of languages spills out of the playbox: here is the variety of codes to which the growing child is exposed. Reaney presents them, as they touch the language-learning child's awareness; each being of equal value and potential to the development of language and understanding—and poetry. The prominence of this theme of discovering poetry makes *Colours in the*

Dark such an interesting text in which to contemplate strategies for presenting the child's world on stage: the patterns of language which Reaney emphasizes are particularly significant in a play so definitely *about* finding language. Among the varied verbal forms, three are especially important to the link between the broad theatrical imitation of play itself, and the actual words which form Reaney's script. The lists of names, the folk poem, and the recurring and expanding "Existence Poem," underpin the child language of *Colours in the Dark*, the first two quite directly, and the "Existence Poem" as a summary of the central movement of the play.

But to show the relevance of these I must first mention the dramatic context in which they occur. *Colours in the Dark* has six central characters from three generations: Pa, Ma, Gramp, Gram, Son, Niece. The actors taking these parts are each expected to play many characters, *"suggesting how we are many more people than just ourselves"* and *"everyone is a multiple character."*[4] Reaney's play does not probe unique psychologies and conflicting motivations. His dramatic language is intended to create types, often from an ironic or satiric perspective. Reaney imitates, then, a child playing through adopting roles: "you be the mommy; I'll be the daddy." In this situation, the characters can be expected to speak relatively little and in relatively few identifying phrases. As Ronald Huebert describes it, there is something of "the medieval *Everyman*" in Reaney's characterizations: "the child-poet of these plays can feel the effects of the two worlds (Innocence and Experience) only as symbolic alternatives, not as dramatic conflict."[5] Reaney puts the audience in the position of watching very young children at such role-playing: an unusual amount of sympathetic and energetic imagining (and, perhaps, great patience) is demanded. Reaney's title, indeed, reminds us that his audience is, literally, in the position of the boy with measles in a darkened room, watching colours in the dark; the play begins with the house lights up and then plunges the audience into darkness.

The form of the play, the apparent raison d'efre for the play, repeatedly emphasizes the child's imaginative freedom to create roles with few props or costumes, and challenges the audience, in the dark in each individual's head, to fill in the colours. The play opens with three child's games: a boy circling the stage on a bicycle, Musical Chairs, and a birthday party version of blindman's buff. When, in the last game, Father is shown to have the talent to "see with his fingers" (15)—identifying characters, predicting vocations, and recognizing colours while blindfolded—the play's narrative line begins as Father's explanation of how he developed such extrasensory, intuitive, and multi-sensory perception. The rest of the play is a telling, by this boy-man whose "mind and heart lines are joined" (13), about how he "became skillful at telling" (15), that is at extrarational understanding.

Reaney establishes, then, a dramatic ploy, which, however random and

free-ranging it is, emphasizes his speculation about imitating play itself. His
strategy is to act out a story within a play, and to make that story a series of
abruptly shifting mini-plays, whose duration reflects the child's limited
concentration on one role. *Colours in the Dark* is a play made up of the
plays in one's life, a playful play about playing. We are, writes G.D. Parker,
"to discover, or recover, something of our own creative power—a power
which originates in the simple *act* of looking and listening."[6] We are to
participate in the language of the sandbox, or of the child's dress-up game, a
language characterized by mimicking a few colloquial scraps which label
each type, much falling out of character, and much excited repetition. If, as
Reaney's descriptions of the play suggest, the script is akin to egocentric
speech, or collective monologues, we have certain clues as to how to
approach the text of the play.[7] The language is first an accompaniment and
reinforcement of action rather than an attempt to communicate; it is
addressed to or centred on the self, or, in L. S. Vygotsky's phrase, it is
" 'speech on its way inward,' "[8] unsuitable in some ways to the very outward
and public demands of theatrical language. The audience is placed in the
unaccustomed position (as far as the theatre is concerned) of overhearing
and enjoying the child's creative play with language.

A play about playing is also, Reaney notes, a collection of short plays,
recitations, and musical performances reminiscent of a Christmas concert at
a country school. Thus, one play often follows another without connection,
transition, though Reaney's Jungian enthusiasm suggests that there are
meaningful unconscious links between apparently random performances.
The playing with plays, and the language accompanying action, reaches its
limit in the second and third sections of Act 2. Within the framework
already established, of a series of plays explaining the poetic father's ability
to play, the Hermit presents his own play within a play. The actors on stage
actually discuss the representation of their play, making the audience freshly
aware of the pretending and of the analogy to children playing at playing.
This scene also marks, apparently, a stage in the "story" of the play, the
child's moving from spontaneous play to self-conscious acting.

For *Colours in the Dark*, whatever its playfulness and inwardness,
perhaps *because* of their primacy, is a play about growing up, about "a man
remembering his life, being initiated into finding some pathway through it,
his finding out how many colours and selves he broke up into, his finding
out how both hostile and loving the most normal figures in one's life could
be" (83). Although it is easy to recognize many of the stages—from a first
job early in the play to a cocktail party near the end—along life's pathway, it
is difficult to identify the stages in language acquisition which might mark
the "hero's" growth. Dominating, and often obscuring, the narrative line of
the play is Reaney's insistence on playing with play. He keeps circling back to

birth, baby, young child, more preoccupied with the repetition and randomness of play than with a line of development. The recurrence of the lists, and the folk poetry, reminds us that the drift of the play is toward a discovery that will keep the child alive within the adult. This child's growing up will result in a "grown-up" child.[9] The language that is acquired in *Colours in the Dark* is, after all, a language of poetry (such as we see developing in the "Existence Poem") a fact of which we are frequently reminded by the play's incorporating a collection of Reaney's own previously published poems.

Indeed, the play might in some ways be better described as a "poem for voices." Yet it is impossible to imagine *Colours in the Dark* being successfully presented as a radio play, in the way we can readily imagine, or recall, fine sound recordings of plays from Shakespeare to Pinter. My focus here on the play as a text in words can only provide an inkling of how Reaney's playful use of lighting, props, slides, and the full resources of the theatre might affect our appreciation of that text.

In the playbox is a collection of objects which speak their own language; they become symbols of some experience, itself complex and elusive, in a person's past. At the same time, *Colours in the Dark* frequently evokes the child's first encounter with an object, the touching of it, the turning over, the smelling, the tasting, and eventually the naming. Thus a very primitive act of thought is involved in the perceiving of the giant paper flowers at the beginning or of the Toronto coat of arms near the end. Indeed, I frequently sense in the play's choric chanting an element of nominal realism, where the word is understood by the very young child as an inherent attribute of the object to which it refers.[10] Throughout the play we are also reminded of the great meaning which rests in objects, outside of language. In Part 10 of Act 1 Reaney pulls a cup out of the playbox and with its help remembers the whole set of dishes, the generations it represents, and the stories it contains. The series of tantalizingly spare sentences that accompany this reflection—"In 1879 a saucer broke." (39)—themselves point up the vividness of a child's perception of an object, or experience, when articulation does not intervene.

Colours in the Dark also takes us to the limits of spoken language. In the pivotal university classroom scene, it is not Sal's skill in using her language which is so powerful, but rather her unlearned talent to speak in tongues, in languages unknown to her, in languages which have disappeared. What is there in language (what emotion, what music) beyond, or before, semantics? Reaney's potential poet must reach for an answer to this question. But Reaney does not allow the play to dissolve into gibberish.

The French theoretician Antonin Artaud had diagnosed the modern theatre's malaise as "a rupture between things and words, between things and the ideas and signs that are their representation"; the cure he proposed was to do away with conventional language altogether. But Reaney, as a poet, was committed to another remedy: he wanted to tie things and ideas and words even closer together, in a new metaphorical configuration, a new zodiac.[11]

In *Colours in the Dark*, the intuitive and spontaneous representations and collisions which occur in the unlighted room are made into pattern, are made richer, through language. Thus, at its simplest, when at the beginning of the play the screen "*lights up with all sorts of colours*," the cast whispers all together "Colours in the dark" (16). The articulation establishes an awe, and a celebration, even some humour, which would not exist without the words.

As a description, or a metaphor, for art, the idea of colouring in the dark suggests a writer's random, instinctual, and perhaps blurred choice of words. Like most poets who play with words, Reaney shows a good deal more design and designing than "scribbling" suggests. And yet the scribbling child is for Reaney a key to an adult's discovery. Especially in the encyclopedia or list, in the folk poem, and in his own existence poem, he sustains the child's perception throughout his play.

The playbox, Reaney tells us in the production notes, contains "a whole life" and, indeed, "all of life." Everywhere in Reaney's work an encyclopedic impulse builds the notion of a world in a playbox. Perhaps the tendency is most pronounced in *Colours in the Dark*, which is divided into sections encompassing the colours of the spectrum, the days of the week, the flowers of the seasons, the visible planets, and the hymns and songs of a culture. Apparently a series of progressions and a whole series of circular structures underlie the play and give it a cyclical and apocalyptic shape. But the symmetries probably make their impression on the audience's subconscious, or on the reader, while the conscious mind in the theatre is more aware of the randomness of play. For instance, the structural principles are implied in lists at the beginning of each colour-phase of the play; Act 2, for example, begins at mid-week with Mother's recitation: "Yellow is for Wednesday, swallowtail butterfly, JKLM, the planet Venus" (65). In part these lists may be strategies for remembering, a kind of *insistence* on system. Yet rather than being in a rainbow, yellow is here in a list with butterfly, Venus, and four letters of the alphabet. In these and the many other lists in the play, Reaney seems to be suggesting something encyclopedic about play language, and child language. An early stage of language acquisition is implied, the elemental one of acquiring vocabulary. Here is the delight of words before syntax, before the combining stage, where the connections between one word and the next exist somewhere in the air, or hidden in the mind, or in the unconscious rather than in the externalization of syntactical glue. The connections are metonymic, the constructions vertical. The basic structure of the play is synchronic rather than diachronic. In *Listen to the Wind* (1972) a list of nine dogs is followed by a chorus of the different barks of each kind. Newfoundland names are chanted and mimed antiphonally in *Geography Match* (1973). *Names and Nicknames* (1973) is the quintessential expression of Reaney's dramatic use of the list as a feature of child language. That play originates in "suites of words used in a speller that my father learned to spell out in the 1890's."[12] In some cases Reaney uses a list of words that belong to the same conceptual category, like that of dogs. More often, he is attracted to lists of a more arbitrary nature, usually with that magic power of names, such as the list of train stations between Stratford and Toronto, or Toronto and Winnipeg in *Colours in the Dark*. The lists provide a found and accidental syntax, rather than an imposed authorial connection.

Furthermore, the list, which isolates single words in turn, again suggests the one-word sentence stage of construction, as well as the language of the child at play. Each word is a world in itself, and the words are learned as an accompaniment to action, as part of the process of interacting with the world. In a Reaney play a single word can be acted; as an initial stage direction to *Names and Nicknames* puts it: "Not every word gets a gesture and the whole thing must be kept flowing, but the actors do say these words with their bodies as well as their mouths."[13]

My daughter, at age nine, loved to list the names of all her friends and their families and recite them to herself. Reaney realizes the power of names (and nicknames), which a nine-year-old will draw on, to shape personality, to give definition, to establish connections. Here is part of the list of fifty-two names of ships (one for each week?) which have brought immigrants to Canada:

Dancing Feather	Flying Foam
Diadem	Gypsy Bride
Early Morn	Go Ask Her
Essence of Peppermint	Glad Tidings (46)
Eva Lynch	

That the list is to be chanted, sung solo and in unison reinforces the significance of its syntax (the units are related by contiguity rather than similarity) in the child language of *Colours in the Dark*. A ship named *Diadem* has a regal personality very different from the impatient freedom of the *Flying Foam*. The list seems to invite the audience to consider such possibilities in each name. And we can readily imagine the miming actions with which the child/actor might reinforce, and develop, each significance. But the list, as well, builds little poems: the developing ballet choreography of *Dancing Feather* and *Diadem*, the bathroom ritual of *Early Morn* and *Essence of Peppermint*.

In rehearsing lists, the child is playing at learning language, is discovering, through creating, both communal and personal significances in words. In catalogues of professions, cocktail party types, or street names, Reaney taps into the dynamism of child language: with the great help of pure chance, an arbitrary list of words will not only bring accommodation to the world, but will free the imaginative processes. The lists contribute to an implication of child language that surfaces in almost every author I have discussed in this book. In an important way, *Colours in the Dark* is a play about unlearning. The categorization and division of the world which is implicit in the process of language learning is then unlearned by eliminating or altering the categorization. This impulse is crucial in the dozens of lists, some very long, in *Colours in the Dark*. The same inclination to a primitive apprehension of language is heard, no doubt, in the folk poems Reaney cherishes. The list of ships is recited while a sea-shanty is heard in the background. The chorus which ends Act 1 is both a list with the disruptive quality I have mentioned, and a poem which provides, like folk poetry, a rhythmical formulation for remembering:

It Takes
The Remembering
Of   four   seasons
Eight   Stars
Sixteen   Sunsets
Thirty-two   Wind whistles
Sixty-four   Dewdrops in the sunrise
One hundred and twenty-eight Trembling leaves
Two hundred and fifty-six   Pebbles
Five hundred and twelve   Snowflakes
One thousand and twenty-four   Cloud shadows
To make one soul   (63)

Folk verse can be defined in two ways. It is verse written by people with no formal, and probably little informal study of poetry and poetics. In this sense, the folk poet is the literary equivalent of the Sunday afternoon painter, essentially naïve about his craft. Another concept of folk poetry emphasizes the audience, or perhaps we can say, the *users* of the poetry. Folk verse is shared and often memorized by members of a community and often accompanies community ritual. Folk poetry, in this sense, can range from Psalm 23 to John MacRae's "In Flanders Fields." Folk poetry in both these senses is a crucial aspect of the child language of *Colours in the Dark*: it is collective, often apparently spontaneous, more oral than written, and, in its technical features, simple and frequently naïve. Perhaps only in its tendency to the didactic does it differ sharply from the cadenced playground lore— exclusive to children, almost tribal—which Iona and Peter Opie so massively catalogued in *The Lore and Language of Schoolchildren*.[14]

Louis Dudek, although he is himself extremely ambivalent about how to react to this aspect of Reaney's work, at first expresses the strongest negative response. Remarking on Reaney's probable inspiration in the "childish doggerel" of William Blake, and the "bathos" of "hymn-book quatrains," Dudek nearly sweeps all Reaney's poetry away as "quite embarrassing": "it is one thing to write *for* children . . . but quite another to be childish or stylistically insipid in a work written for adults."[15] Dudek here seems unwilling to allow what is clearly essential to Reaney's strategy in *Colours in the Dark*: the naïve and childlike breaks down the professional ideas of poetry which Dudek expresses and the audience is presumed to hold. Discovery through play is impossible if play is burdened with rules about its outcome.

Thus *Colours in the Dark* is an encyclopedia of folk poetry as it is of flowers. Children berry-picking make up a poem of names to accompany their play-work (31), and chant as they play their games: "Read our palms. Guess who we are" (12). Schoolyard rhymes are flung back and forth: "The Catholic brats, they don't like cats./They don't eat meat on Friday." (51).[16] The mosaic of folk poems is extended, furthermore, by the many songs and hymns used in the play. In ranging from shanty to Orphan Annie's theme song, *Colours in the Dark* has a good deal in common with popular musical theatre. It is a collage of songs and hymns, weaving in and out, and often presented in reprise (e.g., p. 54). The very familiarity of the pieces gives them their importance as an expression of community. The folk poem is not only powerful in its appeal to togetherness, but as Reaney's parallel with the Christmas concert suggests it is also a combination of the eternally ritual and the profoundly local. People go to the Christmas concert who would never go to the "theatre"; people love folk poems who would never read a "poem." The democratic and regional impulse in the folk poem helps to free Reaney's audience into play.

Insofar as *Colours in the Dark* is about growing up to be a poet, and about the artist growing into an understanding of his art, the folk poetry appears especially interesting. Not only does the collage of poems point to the poetry of a child's spontaneous language play, but the conjunction of naïve verse and Reaney's own previously published poetry implies an articulation, or a defence, of his sort of poetry. The untutored verse I have in mind when I refer to folk poetry is particularly prone, by its very naïveté, to certain features which reveal its primitive or childlike quality. Some obvious examples are very simple rhyme schemes, repetition of a limited repertoire of rhyme words, make-rhymes which make little sense, what we might call make-sense diction which detracts from rhythm or rhyme, and prose rhythm/syntax offered up as poetry. The essence of the genre is found early in the play when Pa, in his guessing at identities, starts to make up a poem on the spur of the moment:

> —An odd little boy who came to school
> And lives in the cemetery
> His mother is a gravestone, his father a
> ghoul
> But we don't mind that very
> At mathematics he's awfully smart
> His backbone's useful to count on
> And I think it's because he's got no heart—
> —I can't think up anymore. (14)

Pa's first poem starts out quite rhythmically, and with an insightful, unusual rhyming of "school" and "ghoul." But the spontaneous poet is soon forced to a desperate rhyming of "very" with "cemetery," in a line that is unfinished, and clumsily ambiguous. The poem descends into makeweight adjectives, pronouns, prepositions and conjunctions, a desperation finally acknowledged: "I can't think up anymore."

I doubt that Reaney would call this bad poetry. Perhaps he would call it "good bad poetry," that is bad poetry whose virtues are important. In *Twelve Letters to a Small Town* (1962) Reaney certainly expresses more affection than contempt for those "dear bad poets/Who wrote/Early in Canada/And never were of note."[17] The authentic local taste in their poems has no substitute. Reaney's own poems are hardly of the same genre as Pa's poem; he is a clever, erudite, and often intricate poet. Yet I am constantly struck by the apparent fumbling, by the jamming of an intensely lyric line with a piece of awkward prose syntax, by a crude rhythm, or a lunging rhyme. *Colours in the Dark* seems so central to Reaney's work because it becomes the literary means for him to discover the dramatic voices which speak his poems, the means for him to hear their childlike crudeness, their folksy naïveté, their spontaneity, their being composed almost line-by-line, by turns, in a group on a wagon travelling into town. Thus part of Reaney's *Twelve Letters to a Small Town*, "Ninth Letter: Town House and Country Mouse" is, within the play, begun by the protagonist/poet, Father, but is *"passed around"* to Gram and Gramp as the buggy heads to town. Thus the clichés ("In another world altogether"), or the documentary counting ("Past the ten huge willows, the four poplars"), or the anticlimax and broken rhythm of the last line ("A dixie-cup of ice cream with a wooden spoon")(57-58), are not only aspects of the boy's wondering voice, but are revealed in the play as the language of his parents, the poetry of the home-place inherited.

In this context, James McIntyre's poem "Ode on the Mammoth Cheese," fits perfectly. Here is an actual folk poem, showing all the vigour and amusing fumbling of the genre:

> Cows numerous as a swarm of bees,
> Or as the leaves upon the trees
> It did require to make thee please
> And stand unrivalled, queen of cheese. (60)

Thus the slack prosiness of "The Royal Visit," which backs up and starts again: "And although/But although"; or the filling up of the rhyme in "The Killdeer": "Uncle Good and Aunt Evil/Took me in, how do you do," (83) are seen in a different light.[18] They are the authentic voices of the child, and of the childlike rural folk. They share, or should share, the sincerity of McIntyre's "Ode." Like the Gothic melodramas and Disney cartoons that Reaney also loves, the ballads, folk poems, and child verse in *Colours in the Dark* are a protest against the categorizing, rational mind, an insistence by example on the freedom, fertility and "relaxed awareness" that comes with imaginative play. Furthermore, in the pervasively symbolic world of Reaney's writing, the folk poem, though not as polished as a piece by Emily Dickinson, or as complex as a poem by T.S. Eliot, may be valued precisely for its simplicity. Here, in the spontaneity of play, perhaps, is not so much novelty of insight, as a clear view of the unconscious, a relatively direct presentation of the symbolic language of the imagination.

If Reaney discovers, or creates, within *Colours in the Dark*, a poetic based on the spur-of-the-moment spoken poems of children and Souwesto rural folk, it is no surprise to find several elements of naïve verse in the "Existence Poem," which Reaney tells us *"ties the whole play together"* (27). The most noticeable of these is the building of a poem from the steady repetition of elementary syntactic structures—"He gives to me a . . .," and "The [subject] is . . . ." Another is the self-questioning, thinking-out-loud at the beginning of the poem: "Existence gives to me/What does he give to me" (27). Another is the noticeable slackening of the rhythm in the third stanza as the speaker gives up on rhyme and regularity of metre to add a list, more colloquially and vaguely: "As well as a company of others such as/Sly

Tod, Reverend Jones, Kitty Cradle and so on'' (127). Perhaps a final feature is Reaney's glib use of what Alvin Lee calls "old-fashioned words,"[19] such adjectives as "hopeful" and "faithful," such abstractions as "love" and "patience."

On the other hand, the poem is very symmetrical. It appears in segments throughout the play and appears complete at the end of the work. The key structural element of the play, that is to say, is the child's working toward completion of the whole poem. Existence is a process of learning language, and the language that is learned is, in effect, the child language of the play. *Colours in the Dark* concerns learning to play with language, or to imitate language at play, not the language of market-place or classroom. Reaney's interpretation of the stages of language acquisition is hinted at in this pivotal poem, eventually titled, at the end of the play, "Gifts" (although the poem exists in other versions before the play).

The gifts of existence, defined by the poem, are essentially four. First is the gift of language itself, as evoked in the first stanza of the poem. The exciting stage of first naming is often expressed in a kind of chant, as the first connections are made between the world of objects out there and the sounds that are generated from within. Throughout the play Reaney's lists remind us of the joy of this early achievement in language learning. If there is a negative side to the discovery of the gift of language, it may be evoked both in the typography that sets the words off in solitude, and in the antiphonal, question/answer, format in which stanza one is first performed (27). Thus, Reaney may remind us that language implicitly divides and fragments the world.

Metaphor, of course, is a linguistic way of overcoming this limitation of language. The second stanza of the "Existence Poem" is in some ways the bleakest, the "desert" stanza, perhaps associated with adolescence, but ultimately with all those times in life when the problems, even the minor ones, seem enormous, insurmountable. When the "pebble is a huge dark hill I must climb," there is a sense of challenge, perhaps of Sisyphean absurdity, but most surely of hyperbole. But from the point of view of language learning, the second stanza is a significant development. The speaker is now in command of metaphor and is therefore able to measure his existence, to understand differences and similarities, by its means.

In stanzas three and four of the poem we pass into the stage of symbol-making. The shift from "I" to "he" suggests other voices entering the poem (and, therefore, the validity of other points of view), and also signals the ability to see oneself objectively. At this point objects fade, and people—not individuals, but types—rise in significance. The immediate world of sensory experience makes connection with the vast world of infinite (mental, unconscious) question and meaning. The symbol, communal or personal, Buddha or Balloon, joins the language of documenting particulars, and the permanent language of art. In the play, public and private symbols, often without system, provide both a verbal language and a language of objects. This stage is intelligently summarized by Alvin Lee in the conclusion to his book on Reaney: "the baring of childhood traumata and the concern with the unconscious in his writings . . . are a movement into what Jung called the collective unconscious or into what Blake found when he passed into the impersonal part of his own mind and discovered all minds."[20]

Apparently in Reaney's terms this awareness of generations of types, and of the elements of oneself in all humanity, makes possible faith (98) and hope. This moment of understanding has its most significant demonstration in Part 16 of Act 2 when the protagonist meets a deformed (and, he thinks, less-than-human) child. Through some mysterious intervention of the symbolic green leaf, he is able to fit the child into his conception of self and of being human:

SON: Things you've lost are inside things you don't like.
PA: Yes. I love you. Without feet you walk with your breath. Without hands your body is a giant's hand. I love you.

(116-17)

An understanding, or perhaps one should better say, a faith in symbol, enables a person to find the things he has lost. The finding, in turn, creates new love of others, an awakening to extraordinary abilities which is accomplished through metaphor.

The poem ends, that is, with a return to metaphor. The interpenetration of things, the hidden world, made apprehendable in symbol, makes it possible for a return to the "I," now presumably, more aware. The metaphors are slightly more elaborated, but most significantly, they are reversed. The tenor of the metaphor in stanza two (for example, "the lake") becomes the vehicle of the metaphor at the end of the poem: "The lake calms down . . . to a dewdrop in a flower" (127). The significance of the metaphor equations so triumphantly chanted in Part 9 of Act 2 is here clarified. The poem, and the play, ends at the limit of its playfulness with language. Here is both a way of understanding relationships, and a way of recognizing integration, of recognizing the whole and the infinity of relationships. Each equation now comes back to the individual "I" and presumably enables the Father's own awareness—of the mountain in his own hand, for example. Colours in the Dark is thus a dramatic representation of the awareness born of play. Because the child's play with a few simple words leads to understanding, and often, to unique articulation,

Reaney constructs his play not on a narrative line, or even on symbolic pattern (though both are there to a degree), but as a series of imitations of play, with objects, with music, with images, with other people, and especially, with language. We understand the fleeting glimpse of the Queen of England as more tantalizing than the "queen of cheese"; we see Orphan Annie in "a pink frilly Shirley Temple dress" as more queenly than the "gracious pink figure" in "The Royal Visit"; and reversing the metaphors, we see the "queen of cheese" as more certainly the ruler of its community than the queen of England. The audience chooses, in a spirit of play, to play with connections, not so much those articulated by the playwright as those by chance made available by his own playing. When you can reverse a metaphor, you recognize that language is arbitrary and interchangeable, that its manipulation can bring control of your world—and defiance of the system, the control inculcated by any system of language. You have learned, in mature awareness, to manipulate language in ways which the learning child will do unconsciously. You recognize that it is possible to colour in the dark. A sound uttered where there is no light—the sounds we make when we say "red" or "yellow"—create the most vivid colour, in the mind.

9

Child, Magician, Poet: Playing with the Pre-verbal in Dennis Lee and bill bissett

> *Child, magician, poet*
> *by incantation rule.*
> > Daniel G. Hoffman, "In the Beginning"
>
> *They simplify*
> *who say the Artist's a child*
> *they miss the point closely: an artist*
> *even if he has brothers, sisters, spouse*
> *is an only child.*
> > Les A. Murray, "Portrait of the Autist as
> > a New World Driver."

Among Canadian artists, Dennis Lee and bill bissett are the magician-poets, with a secret knowledge of illusion which can mesmerize large crowds. I think of them as "only" children, in the sense that they do not seem to belong to any of the family groupings in their generation of poets. Lee and bissett are, of course, very different poets—in popularity, audience, reputation, and expression—yet they are also curiously similar: both in the profound way in which the familiar child/artist analogy describes them, and in their empathy with child language.

This chapter approaches closest to the boundaries of my subject. At one limit is nursery rhyme, where the separation between children's literature and children in literature is probably crossed. (Although I do not finally accept the division, this book obviously uses it implicitly.) At the other limit is a single-minded, preoccupied, poetic experimentation, where the line between literature and play is crossed. Perhaps nowhere else in this book am I so aware that any artist worth writing about is too complex, too whole, to be satisfactorily understood through one approach, one chapter, even one book. The Lee of *Alligator Pie*, who is my particular focus in this chapter, is also the most audacious critic of Canadian literature, in *Savage Fields*, and the most searching political poet in Canada, in *Civil Elegies*. And the prolificness, the unpredictability, the ridiculousness, even the triviality, of bill bissett almost defies comment itself, leave alone focus.

I believe, however, that significant insights into these poets are found in considering them as creators of two very different child languages. The difficulty of applying my concepts of literary child languages to poetry, especially to lyric poetry, as shown in the chapter on Page, Livesay, and Waddington, is that we find there no specific child, that is no *character*, against whom we might test the details of the language. Rather, there is usually a childlike persona with no overt character other than that revealed in his self-expression. Vibrating with what we might call the natural autism of the child, Lee and bissett create precious inner worlds out of words, solitary, seemingly self-entertaining magic.

In his comment on writing for children, titled "Roots and Play," Lee emphasizes the inspiration of "Carroll and Milne—master of the lunatic muse, and master of the domestic inward muse."[1] Lee follows these muses in creating a private language, a code in which children can enclose themselves and express a vision different from adults. Like Carroll, he creates a verbal structure which can "be perceived only as what it [is], and not some other thing."[2] In this ambition, at least, bissett resembles Lee; in short, the World of Nonsense, as here paraphrased from Elizabeth Sewell's *The Field of Nonsense* (1952), is vital to both writers:

> The objects manipulated in the game of nonsense are words, and in nonsense the mind uses words so that "its tendency toward order [will] engage its contrary tendency towards disorder, keeping the latter perpetually in play and so in check . . . ." Nonsense uses language so that words and syntax maintain a balance between a disorder of discrete objects entirely without relation to one another, and the coherence and similitudes of dream or poetry.[3]

Fundamental to this game of words is the desire to encounter words as they were before they signified something to us. The crucial impetus in the child language of both Lee and bissett is the attempt to "look at language as children or Lewis Carroll look at language."[4]

Lee and bissett are most obviously linked by this radical looking, this naïve approach to words. They are most obviously different in their audiences. (I am, let me remind you, restricting myself here to Lee's children's poetry.) Lee writes poems for children, first of all; bissett uses a child language as strategy in poems addressed first to adults. Lee's success surely has much to do, too, with his ability to present many of his poems from the child point of view, in a child voice. Our family favourite among these poems is "Tricking," a three-year-old's view of the finish-your-vegetables-first ritual:

> When they bring me a plate
> Full of stuff that I hate,
> Like spinach and turnips and guck,
> I sit very straight
> And I look at the plate
> And I quietly say to it: "YUCK!"[5]

The first great pleasure in the poem is that the three-year-old speaker is in control of the situation, a reversal that appeals both to the child and to the adult reader's sense of the true politics of the situation. In "Peter Rabbit" (55-57), Lee saucily takes Peter's point of view against the orders of his parents. "Thinking in Bed" (40) shows a fine sympathy for the child's emerging sense of identity.

In each case Lee presents his child speaker at play, in the essential games of establishing social relationships, and of exploring language. For Lee, in *Alligator Pie*, no concept is more crucial than play: his ideal is that the poems "play successfully." And in his insistence on play my analogy with the enclosed world of nonsense is evident:

Children play with an absorption and a purity of intent which most adults can only covet. Their play may be trivial or profound, celebratory or cruel. Indeed this is one of the features of play. It can range from a light-hearted release of energy through to high celebration and to joy; as Huizinga says in *Homo Ludens*: "frivolity and ecstasy are the twin poles between which play moves." It is a self-contained activity which allows these impulses their own space, treats them as our proper necessities.[6]

"Someday I'll go to Winnipeg," Lee muses, "To win a peg-leg pig./But will a peg-leg winner win/The piglet's ill-got wig?" (51). This is Lee playing with an absorption and purity of intent which most of us can only covet. The play is completely self-contained, and serves only itself. Lee's tongue-twister is a way of expressing in language the stage prior to language when there were no categories, divisions, concepts, or even named objects: "The one-ing of the world . . . is the essence of lyricism. . . . the perception of a coherence of being.''[7] For Lee this coherence is also implicit in the biological dimension of language, which, again, is particularly evident in child language. The physical articulation of the words, the physicality of rhythm, are crucial to the success of his child poems: "nursery rhymes can't be approached at an adult's reading rate. They unfold much more slowly. In fact, they need to be brought to life almost as tiny plays, preferably with much pulling of faces and bouncing of rear-ends on knees."[8] Lee writes so that such physical action is almost inescapable:

> *With a bump on your thumb*
> *And a thump on your bum*
> *And tickle my tum in Toronto. (23)*

Nowhere is the critic more fearful of comment. Play is not play if we make it consciously purposive. Yet I think it's important to insist here that we are dealing with two writers for whom play is an essential feature of language. Julia Kristeva in her fine, if daunting, definition of poetic language, constantly makes this connection (so marvellously embodied in Lee) to child and biology:

> One should begin by positing that there is within poetic language . . . a *heterogeneousness* to meaning and signification. . . . detected geneti-cally in the first echolalias of infants as rhythms and intonation anterior to the first phonemes, morphemes, lexemes, and sentences . . . . We shall call this disposition *semiotic* . . . in short, a *distinctiveness* admitting of an uncertain and indeterminate articulation because it does not yet refer (for young children) or no longer refers (in psychotic discourse) to a signified object for a thetic consciousness.[9]

As Kristeva explains, in poetic language this semiotic function "tends to gain the upper hand."[10] In Lee—and still more so in bill bissett—a disposition to the pre-verbal features of language is vital. The network connecting them to biology, the child's pre-semantic apprehension of words, and poetry, is relatively explicit in their work. A closer look at sound, syntax, and semantics in Lee, leads us continually back to this network which defines his child language.

In the poem which has become a national, if not international, institution, "Alligator Pie," the aggressive meter, based largely on monosyllables and a large number of strong accents, makes the reader and listener move with the poem: "rhythm in the words, translating itself from the jounce of your knee, through the child's bum and up and down its spine."[11] The quartet of rhyme words (aaaa, bbbbb, etc.) is probably more critical to the success of the poem: it provides the form for perpetuating the poem. As Lee tells us at the end of the book, children are willing poets: "Try starting a verse 'Alligator juice.' " The quadruple rhymes and the caesuras in each line invite children (and the adult!) to sustain and invent rhymes and to create through language, with little attention to meaning in the observable world (how edible is alligator pie?). Lee encourages an approach to the words "before they refer": "words should never be sacred. A rhyme is meant to be used, and that means changing it again and again . . . . If your child inadvertently rewrites some of these poems, please take his version more seriously than mine." (63) Lee has produced, with contemporary and Canadian references, the essentials of all nursery rhyme: "strong rhythm, very clear and definite intonation patterns," "repetitiveness," combined with "relatively unimportant" meaning. Such characteristics provide verbal constructions which, from his very first attempts, the child can produce whole, something that "sound[s] like nursery rhymes although the content [is] not recognisable."[12] Lee wraps his tongue around self-contained patterns of words within which the child can play.

"On Tuesdays I Polish My Uncle" begins with a simple, colloquial, and, until the fourth line, an unexceptional narrative. Each stanza builds on this first stanza, so that we are given both a cumulative and a self-generating poem. Variations in subject, predicate, and, of course, rhyme ("Beans in his jeans, a bee on his knee," 47) become means for making successive poems within the same poem. The poem encourages the child because it is an externalization of his own process of language investigation and development: "the joining stage is fully in hand when putting words together becomes a form of play. There is much self-directed repetition; children's monologues sometimes sound like students doing pattern drills in a language lab."[13]

The incantatory refrains in many of Lee's poems are, of course, one example of such playful drill. But the intricate self-enclosed, nonsense monologue, "The Sitter and the Butter and the Better Batter Fritter," is a more elaborate example. Playing with the possibilities of the "syllable + ter suffix" combination, Lee uses only actual words in English, but in a sense he needn't: the combinations of sounds, outside of meaning, are essential. The poem practises a particular range of articulation. But also, like incantation generally, the poem tends to induce a sort of hypnotic state, beyond, or prior to, meaning. A student of child language would also remark that the alliterated "b" is a second key element in the self-generation of this poem. We know that voiced consonants are the child's first choice for the beginnings of words, and that a child will routinely replace unvoiced consonants (/p/, /t/, and /k/) with voiced counterparts (/b/, /d/, /g/) at the beginnings of words.[14] The bemusing barrage of ''b's'' in this poem is Lee's instinctive recognition of this feature of child language.

For a description of the syntax in Lee's child language, we find some useful direction in the psycholinguist's description of motherese, or caretaker language. The features of motherese give us a good beginning for a description of nursery rhymes in general—themselves a kind of caretaker language. Alison Elliot summarizes its characteristic modifications of adult speech: (1) paralinguistic features: high pitch, exaggerated intonation; (2) syntactic features: shorter mean length of utterance, fewer verb forms and modifiers, fewer subordinate clauses/embeddings per utterance, shorter mean preverb length, more verbless utterances, more content words, fewer function words; (3) discourse features: more interrogatives and imperatives, speech more fluent and intelligible, more repetitions whether complete, partial or semantic.[15] Of these, certainly the high proportion of content words, in, for example, ''On Tuesdays I Polish My Uncle,'' the fewer verb forms and modifiers in a poem such as ''Ookpik'' (21), and the lack of subordinate clauses (''In Kamloops,'' 17; ''Billy Butter,'' 18-19) are obvious in Lee's poems. Many of the poems are based on a short four-, five-, or six-syllable line, and, as we have seen, longer lines, such as those in ''Alligator Pie,'' are divided by caesurae into short utterances. A few poems, most notably ''Bouncing Song'' (10), are lists with very few verbs.

It's also worth noting, however, when speaking of syntax, that within the dominant playfulness that rules Lee's compositions, an occasional deviation from standard syntax is used, it seems, to signal the child's talk. The very young speaker (still in a crib) in ''The Special Person'' is immediately marked in the second line of the poem by a syntactical redundancy, a triple designation of location:

> I've got a Special Person
> At my day-care, where I'm in.
> Her name is Mrs. Something
> But we mostly call her Lynn. (24)

A different syntactical variation marks the speaker in ''Tricking'':

> Little kids bawl
> Cause I used to be small,
> And I threw it all over the tray. (32)

The marvellous effectiveness of this poem is here revealed: the tricking even extends to tricking with language. The speaker's syntax indicates cause and effect, though none is apparent. Lee suggests, here, a stage of language use which is technically labelled " 'naïve psychology' where the child sprinkles his speech with logical connectives, such as *if* and *because*, which give a spurious impression of logical thought but which do not guarantee adequate understanding of their semantic implications."[16] The stage is also revealed, as we shall see again in bissett, through the relentless use of the (less logical) connective "and," which gives an impression of accumulation but often without evident relationships.

In both these cases, to be sure, what I have called syntactic deviations serve first the dictates of metre and rhyme. But, in Lee's pervasive sympathy for the child's language, expressed in his insistence on the value of the rhyme the child creates or of the word he alters, even the sound patterns can be sacrificed. At the end of "Tricking," for example, Lee suddenly violates the pattern of the poem, ending on a 6- instead of an 8-syllable line, and putting the rhyme in an awkward two-syllable word, rather than in the monosylla- bles that, except in one instance, carry the rhyme throughout the poem. The point seems to be that metre or rhyme, like words, must not be sacred. In skipping songs, like "Singa Songa" (10) and "Mumbo, Jumbo" (13), and in several other instances, Lee ends with a similar anticlimactic deviation. The poems ends with a thud, but the child language—the not-quite-successful attempt to maintain the regular pattern—seems authentic, its naïveté part of Lee's carefully won effect.

In this discussion, I have already suggested something of Lee's diction, especially the necessity of concrete words. Everything, like alligator pie, is countable, and very specific in image content; it's almost impossible to find an abstraction, except the nearly tangible "nothing" in "Ookpik" (21). Beyond this rather obvious feature (much of modern poetry can be similarly described), the most important aspect of Lee's diction is its inventiveness; he plays with the sounds and connectiveness of language, and he encourages his listener/reader, we have already noted, to participate in the play of coinage.

One of the great appeals of Dr. Seuss, it's always seemed to me, is that where received language runs out, the voice creates a word: the poetry is productive, it suggests crib language, where the child is testing possibilities. So, too, with Lee, though in a less exaggerated way than in Dr. Seuss:

> It isn't me,
> It isn't you,
> It's nutty, mutty
> Psychapoo. (44)

Here, as with the "grundiboob" in "If You Should Meet," and with figures in a half-dozen other poems, Lee coins a name for a fantasy character. Moreover, and more significantly, there is the coinage "mutty" which has no meaning, except the profound meaning of nonsense. So, too, for "willoughby, wallaby, woo" (15), "higgledy piggledy/Sniggledy sneezle" (39), and the rest. Lee takes his reader, or, better listener, into the realm of language for language's sake, that is not into gibberish but into the experience of originating language. This is a language which, although not found in a dictionary, serves many of the crucial functions of language—expressing emotion, drawing attention to oneself, even labelling. And, of course, the neologisms also make some conventional meaning in their differentiation from the sound of a familiar word: the intersection of "nutty" and "mutt" in "mutty," for example.

In his use of place names, Lee also taps into this sense of a language originating. Without rejecting the traditional nursery rhymes, Lee remembers his first impulse to write child's poetry in the difference: "they were no longer home ground" (63). The poems of *Alligator Pie* become home ground and particularly appealing to Canadians, in their use of place names; that is, Lee is connecting with the first naming which makes a language for, a home out of, a particular space. He makes a political gesture through his repeated appeal to the primitive process of naming:

> In Kamloops
> I'll eat your boots.
>
> In the Gatineaus
> I'll eat your toes. (17)

And so on. Here the child's very early labelling of the parts of the body—which is the beginning of his verbal definition of self—is implicitly joined to the naming of the body politic of which he is a part. Moreover, this is an example of a poem which invites the child to add more verses, more body parts, more names, through the play of sound; thus, the poem can define each child's own community, even outside Canada: "You should feel free to relocate the place-poems as drastically as you want. Put in the streets and places you know best; the rhyme and the metre may get jostled a bit, but so what?" (63)

Conventionally naming defines, and separates. But Lee's continual tendency toward a feeling for language before it refers may also originate in naming. A short poem best illustrates this opposite side of naming:

> If I lived in Temagami,
> Temiskaming, Kenagami,
> Or Lynx, or Michipicoten Sound,
> I wouldn't stir the whole year round

> Unless I went to spend the day
> At Bawk, or Nottawasaga Bay,
> Or Missinabi, Moosonee,
> Or Kahshe or Chicoutimi. (50)

On the one hand, "Kahshe or Chicoutimi" is the most relentless example of Lee's celebration of the intimate link between names and a sense of identity (interestingly, most of these names, if not all, originate in indigenous languages, prior to the English language's naming of the continent). On the other hand, Lee is once again at play with language, prior to reference, where the effect veers toward nonsense. Another description of nonsense, here describing Lee's beloved Lewis Carroll, also serves to describe this poem:

> Generally, we use proper nouns as pointers and nothing more. Poetry makes much use of this, using them where possible as series of lovely sounds but not entirely devoid of reference or at least of connections, since they have associational power if not much in the way of content . . . . The names in Nonsense are not nothingnesses; they work by association, as the names in poetry do, but their associations are with words.[17]

Lee's poetry finds its power in such originating language—in language regarded as sound prior to reference, in the child's invented words, in the country's naming itself, and in the language play his verse not only imitates but skilfully invites. One traditional device of poetry, the metaphor, has, consequently, little place in Lee. Whatever "creating" metaphor is, it is not, except unintentionally, a part of child language.[18] There are few poems in *Alligator Pie* that have anything approaching a metaphor in them. Where we do find something that we might be tempted to label metaphor—"And every time/He heard a shout,/He took his pencil/And rubbed it out." (44)—we quickly realize that the speaker conceives, and the reader (both child and adult) responds only to the *literal* interpretation. We are, in other words, at the first level of metaphoric understanding, prior to mature comprehension, suitably called *magical*: for the child encountering metaphor, "the interpretation is made literal by the mental construction of a suitable scenario."[19] In one poem, again thinking/talking like a child, Lee makes the magic of literalism explicit:

> Skyscraper, skyscraper,
> Scrape me some sky:

> Tickle the sun
> While the stars go by. (30)

Here is another confirmation of what we have seen throughout this discussion: Lee makes fine poems for children because he is in tune with the child's language, and here with the different, and magical, child's comprehension of language's inherent connections.

Among the writers I have discussed, bill bissett least often makes childhood and children an explicit subject. Yet bissett must be the creator of the purest child language in Canadian literature. Let me illustrate with an example from the opening lines of "th tempul firing":

> fires in th tempul
> wind in th tempul
> fires round th tempul
> air in th tempul
> sings in th tempul
> fires in th tempul
> rings of th tempul
> skys in th tempul
> water is th tempul
> in th tempul sun is th sun in th tempul[20]

Compare bissett's poem with an actual recorded example of a child's (age 2½) bedtime monologue; the items are excerpted from a sequence of just over forty utterances:

> What color
> what color blanket
> what color map
> what color glass
>
> . . .
>
> red ant
> fire
> like lipstick
>
> . . .
>
> blanket
> now the blue blanket
>
> . . .
>
> what color TV
> what color horse

then what color table
then what color fire
. . .
here yellow spoon[21]

These inner speeches might be the voices of two "only children," in their enclosed solitudes celebrating, combining, testing. Both play variations on a single phrase, both generate sequences of words through aural associations, both explore different uses and contexts of two or three key words, both even use semantic units of nearly the same length. Perhaps the key point of this analogy is that bissett's play, like all play, involves an enormous amount of repetition. The repetition, with slight variation, which is the form of the child's monologue, would be thought, in most writers for adults, to be quickly tiresome. Not so for bissett: for him, there is a necessity in repetition, far beyond that we have observed in Lee (or in poetry, generally), which emerges in aspects of bissett's sound, spelling, visualization, syntax, and diction.

Looking at these two "poems" together makes the case for describing bissett's as child language, the most sustained writing I know of that might carry this description. I am not suggesting that bissett is only childish, or that he consciously sets out to write crib talk (however accurately the eternal child defines his public image).[22] As with each of our subjects, some kind of child language is a strategy to express the writer's own complex vision, and his sense of what poetry/fiction is. Among other things, for example, bissett's manner suggests extreme romanticism, in which some form of child sensibility is an expression of disgust with "the emergd middul class" and "th technicians of a fragmented society" (44). But, as fundamental as "child language" is to bissett, he is, finally, suspicious even of child language, which is, after all, a language in accelerated process, progressing toward accommodation with the too rigid patterns of the received and conformity-inducing prestige dialect. He would like, I think, to "help th children destroy even those/patterns yu place upon their undrstandings" (28).

Bissett, presumably, aims to express a vision prior to, or beyond, these patterns. Like Lee he seeks to create an atmosphere in which words are received as if they did not refer. Yet clearly bissett's play is both more radical and more unswervingly maintained than Lee's. The crucial difference is that Lee attempts to liberate his child reader/listener into language, and bissett attempts to liberate his adult reader/listener from language. Lee tries to get the child playing; bissett conveys the pleasure of his own play. Bissett's aim is perhaps also defined by Kristeva in her comment on such "difficult" modern writers as Céline, Artaud, or Joyce. They oblige the reader, she writes, "to shatter his own judging consciousness in order to grant passage through it to this rhythmic drive constituted by repression and, once filtered by language and its meaning, experienced as jouissance." Certainly the experience of jouissance, of a sensual, sometimes almost orgasmic delight, seems to be the effect of bissett's chanting, rattle-shaking performances. And Kristeva's wan question might equally fit the frequent reaction to bissett: "Could the resistance against modern literature be evidence of an obsession with meaning, of an unfitness for such jouissance?"[23]

No writer in Canada is an easier target for the charge of meaninglessness. Some of his books are so poorly printed, or reproduced, that they are almost impossible to see/read. (On the other hand, in the context of this discussion, I recognize how much a book like *(th) Gossamer Bed Pan* resembles, in individual collages, and in the randomness of the whole, a child's scrapbook/ play book.)[24] Moreover, bissett is unable, apparently, even to spell. The bizarreness of his orthography is the most obvious feature of his child language. In his refusal to follow conventions of spelling and capitalization, bissett makes a superficial—but variously significant—protest against the homogeneous society. It is the training to conformity that bissett defies: see, you can understand me just as well, even when I don't follow the rules— what, then, is the point of the rules?

But there is, of course, more to bissett's spelling than politics. In generally following an informal phonetic transcription he focuses attention on the oral aspect of language. Furthermore, words such as "pome" (poem) or "cummin" (coming), move the poem away from the written (and socially prestigious) toward the spoken and colloquial (and sacred): bissett, that is, is spelling the way people talk, and in the voice of the average person. Similarly, by eliminating many vowels—"th," "whn," etc.—bissett shows the slurring, hurried impression of everyday speech. In familiar conversation the definable meanings of words are often irrelevant: bissett's spelling shows both the conventionality in language and the various non-semantic ways in which language means.

This point returns us to the subject of child language. A child communicates fluently years before he can spell. When he does begin to spell he makes many of the "mistakes" that bissett employs—that is, he follows primarily phonetic principles, rather than conventions. The spelling, itself, insists on our apprehending language before it has become rigidified in the standard dialect: bissett's spelling is a visual means of moving the reader to a stage prior to language, to genuinely experiencing a word anew, as if encountered for the first time. Another crucial effect of this child language is that such phonetic spelling breaks language down into phonemes, makes us aware of the units of sound rather than the meaning. Bissett makes this general effect visually obvious in poems where he uses the lines of the poem to separate the syllables of a single word, as in "ta rattul," which breaks down the word, to form visually the handle of the rattle:

raa
tul
raa
tul   (65)

Bissett thus evokes, perhaps, a more universal language: at the babbling stage, where an infant is experimenting with a range of sounds rather than words, children of different backgrounds all sound alike.[25] None of this is to deny that bissett achieves more conventional effects by his spelling. To pun by consistently spelling "do" as "dew" is to evoke a sense of a freshness, fluidity, and gentleness of dawning, which would not otherwise belong to the commonplace verb. Nevertheless, the presiding effect is not of semantic resonance so much as of an absolutely elemental look at the components of language, before meaning. Perhaps no poet is less comfortable with the conventions of the printed page: bissett is the sound poet par excellence. He must be heard, shaking his rattles, bouncing fluidly from heel to toe, for one to appreciate the way in which his work is so fundamentally child language, that is language before concept, meaning and image, even language before speech. Much of his poetry is pure sound:

ya ankuua chayunakanee
yaa eee unee ka cha tu
yee ka anee kee kee whunajee u (68)

"Gibberish," the frustrated reader mutters at this point, and hastens back to Donne or Keats. And I would not want to call him back to argue that a meaning—as conventionally understood—had been missed. But again, one crucial aspect of a child's language learning provides an instructive analogy. "Six- to eight-month-old infants from an English-speaking background readily distinguish phonemic contrasts in Hindi and Salish. . . . When they were tested again at the age of 12 months, the same infants, like English-speaking adults, did not detect the contrasts to which they had earlier been sensitive." This is striking experimental support for an apparently sentimental platitude, that a child has superior knowledge (in one dimension) and greater openness to other cultures. "It appears that perceptual horizons narrow as a child learns his or her native language."[26] Bissett has made not a single gesture, but a career-long effort to sustain in himself and revive in his audience inactive perceptual mechanisms still available to us.

In many other sound poems in which bissett uses identifiable words, the effect is more like echolalia than meaning. One such poem repeats the line, "what we dew if thrs anything we dew is to take care uv/th erth" (58), in various continually shorter units. In such charged incantation—again one needs to hear the poem "performed"—the speaker repeats the sounds so insistently that both he and his listener are carried into some kind of primitive biological fusion with the natural world. His performance, in a high pitch, with exaggerated intonation and relentless repetition, links him with the voice register of ritual language as well as of child language. The meaning—that there is a deep, unconscious compulsion to protect the world that sustains us—is supported by an unthinking sympathy induced by chant. But for bissett, as for the child, there is always fundamentally, the pleasure of play, the joy of linguistic experiment, before the quasi-religious achievement: "While bissett's sound poems have affinities with Oriental and Amerindian chanting, they are more than imitations. Remarkably, they combine with their reverence or praise the playful quality we often sense in uncodified ritual."[27]

Bissett's radical play with sounds is reinforced not only by the visualness of his private spelling, but also by his attention to the physical appearance of words, letters, and type. Bissett is both sound poet and concrete poet: most of his poems are shaped in some way on the page. Generally the appearance of his poems on the page suggests a biological rhythm, a visual expansion to the margins followed by contraction, like waves on a beach, or a heart beating.[28] At other times he seems to represent instinctively, "th picture inside th/ word."[29] "What we dew" (58) drifts into diminishing streams, as if tiny rivulets of words were forming as the dew disappears. Moreover, many of his poems are accompanied by primitive stick drawings, by the spikey suns, and lollipop flowers, of child art. In the same realm are the collages of comic book images (26) and the concomitant affection for comic book language, particularly for such pre-literate expressions as "bam" or "pow." Like a child with his blocks, bissett often looks at letters as so many pleasing and manipulable shapes, not as components of language. But this is not meant to suggest that there are not marvellous, often joking effects, in his best concrete poems. An untitled poem (63), for example, is entirely composed of the letters "n" and "o," often overtyped to create a silhouette of the parliament buildings, or of some similar public edifice. The letter "n" is perhaps an unknown quantity that nonetheless gives definition to sky and mountain. But blended with "o" it becomes building, a city, a seat of political power, which is *on*, that is superimposed, and yet which is *no*, an aggregation unequivocally rejected.

Such possibilities remind us that the poet's child language is a combination of features presenting a child's vision, and not a total mimicking of early language. In the great majority of bissett's poetry, however, it seems that the poet is talking to himself; his poems are a sort of thinking out loud. Perhaps even his social/political poems are reminiscent of what Piaget called egocentric speech. The most obvious syntactic reflection of such speech is its extreme repetition. In bissett "repetition of words and syllables serving no obvious social function" represents a child whose language is in transition (as his world is in flux), whose personal integrity, manifested in language primarily "individual and self-regulating", is uppermost.[30]

In the excerpt from "th tempul firing," quoted at the beginning of this discussion, for example, there are only two predications, the second of which hardly makes a conventional sentence. But there are ten prepositional phrases ending with "th tempul," eight of which use "in." The poem does not attempt to describe the temple: indeed the pun on the temple of the brain, suggests that the poem might be situated entirely within the head. The internality of the poem certainly reinforces this effect. What we have, then, are variations on a prepositional phrase, variations on that feature of the language designating location and enclosure. It is as if the poet is playing with the possibilities of the phrase in order to discover his own "in-ness," and the possible verbal contexts of a single phrase. But the juxtaposition of images is not purely random; although no conventional syntax connects the lines, the repetition itself, of course, holds the poem together. As for the transitions from line to line, these appear to be made by the playful mind, working from one image to the next. "Fires" leads to "wind," which both promotes and is a result of fire, but "sings" rhymes with "rings." In other words, the criteria for linking things is constantly changing; the poem appears to be an expression of syncretic reasoning, in the pre-school (preconceptual) period, where disparate objects are grouped according to the child's limited, and continually changing, criteria.[31]

Clearly, another effect is associated with such unusual repetition accompanied by none of the conventional syntax of the English sentence. Bissett's syntax provides very little conceptualizing or rationalizing of the world. His child language, rather, carries us readily into the dream-world, or visionary realm, where the biological being, the sensual, the intellectual, the transcendent are unthinkingly fused.

The repetition in bissett's egocentric monologues also tends to focus our attention on what limited conventional syntax can be found. That is, when we hear, or more especially, when we read, the same sentence over and over we begin to study its syntax in spite of ourselves. In many poems such as "what we dew if thrs anything we dew" (58), we are led to consider the construction of particular expressions already mentioned. The poem "i herd ya laffin" consists of the following two lines repeated thirteen times:

i herd ya laffin in th water
i herd ya laffin water (64)

This, again, seems more self-directed monologue than social communication. The singular variation in the sentence turns the reader to contemplating
the syntax (again, interestingly, the function of the prepositional phrase).
Here the dropping of "in th" changes the participial phrase, from
modifying "ya" to modifying "water," or even to an adjective modifying
water—as if the poem were addressed either to "water" or to "laffin water."
The effect, of course, is also to identify you (ya) with water. The poem
resembles a child's syntactical playing, where he is learning that words can
have different relationships, where he is also concentrating on relating himself to himself, rather than on communicating a vision.

Where bissett uses the more conventional syntactical indicators, pronouns
and conjunctions, we often sense they are used without the speaker's fully
understanding their function. He overuses the definite article, as I have
discussed in the introduction. Often we encounter something like this:

nd the kultur thing has bin pretty
well rippd off   but yu cant count on
th weathr   (138)

Here there is an essential conjunction, "but," which suggests a connection
that the reader is at a loss to discover. More aggressively, in "why dew
magazines lie" (39) bissett opens with fourteen "because" clauses, several of
which defy the connection with the question posed in the title. As in Lee, the
spurious logic of naïve psychology seems to be evoked: bissett seems to be
trying to persuade himself of reasons, and connections, which he can't
imagine actually knowing.

If we were to take "i herd ya laffin in th water" as a representative bissett
poem—a more hazardous assumption than with most poets—its seven
words might also tell us something about bissett's poetic vocabulary. He
depends on a commonplace verb, two pronouns, a definite article, a
preposition and a verb as modifier. It is, perhaps, only accidental to my
argument that the *I/you* distinction is the first pronoun distinction to be
mastered by children, and that *in* is apparently the easiest locative
preposition for a child.[32] On the other hand, if the repetition blurs the
distinction between "I" and "you", the confusion is entirely consistent with
the speech of autistic children, and presumably, with bissett's view of an
unfortunate distinction.[33]

Again, as the spelling insists, the poem repeats a scrap of spoken
language: bissett's vocabulary almost always reflects his extremely strong

oral dimension. Indeed, since child language is entirely spoken, this characteristic itself complements the other more specific features I have isolated. Given its orality, and its playful autism, bissett's poetry in general employs a vocabulary less specific, less sensory or imagistic, less colourful perhaps than that of most modern poets. Repetition, of course, limits vocabulary: the contrasting elaboration of a Wallace Stevens, or a Dylan Thomas, or even of an Al Purdy, requires a richly varied and unusual vocabulary. In bissett, an abstraction, like "prayer," because it is relentlessly repeated and spelled "prayr" (suggesting, also, someone who prays), becomes assimilated to the simplified vocabulary (47).

Perhaps no feature of bissett's child language, after spelling, is so obvious as his apparent overuse of the definite article. Since I have discussed this feature in the opening chapter, referring to "yu sing," I will not dwell on the point here. We notice the same feature in "th tempul firing," in "th breath" (153-56), and in many other poems. In child language the definite article is used first for its deictic function (pointing); use of the definite article "to refer to something previously mentioned in the discourse" comes very late, around age nine.[34] Thus, bissett's extensive use of the deictic definite article could be another aspect of his child language, suggesting a sensibility obsessed with directing attention to particular objects (to the integrity of their being), unconcerned with coherence of discourse.

Bissett's vocabulary, broadly speaking, derives from that intermediate level of generality characteristic of a child's early language.[35] Bissett is more likely to speak of "flowers" (49) than of "daffodils or "plants." This inclination again demonstrates the integrity of bissett's vision, where he employs enough categorizing to make elemental distinctions, but a general enough vocabulary to represent an ecological world in which there is so much common need and interdependency.

Bissett's language is not heavily metaphorical. He is, like the child, likely to happen accidentally on metaphor, not to generate metaphor intentionally like most of his fellow poets. His tendency to generate metaphor incidentally, suggests again those primitive stages of metaphorical comprehension known as "magical" and "metonymic."[36] Thus we can imagine the speaker constructing a suitable scenario to explain that the water is literally laughing, or finding them connected by association. Something similar is true of "and th green wind is mooving thru th summr trees" (66), where it seems we are to understand the chant in its magical sense—the wind literally has a colour— rather than in the more sophisticated metaphorical sense of associating certain qualities of green with the wind.

This discussion of bissett's vocabulary may distort the poetry by its emphasis on child language and its ignoring of another staple of bissett's work, the obscenity and the vocabulary, usually colloquial, of sexuality. Yet there may not be as wide a gap between child language and obscenity as we might expect. Kristeva, at least, seems to insist on a close connection, noting that in their not "referring . . . to an object exterior to discourse" obscenities move a discourse away from meaning, in the direction of the jubilant escape from repression that is characteristic of "children's counting-out rhymes."[37] This surprising linking of two codes seems effectively to describe the range of bissett's language.

But the first effect in bissett, even in a poem on an obviously "adult" subject, is that the poet's child language alters our perception of the subject. When Barbara Herrnstein Smith sets out to define the difference between natural and fictive (that is, literary) discourse, she turns, as most linguists do, to the "child's earliest verbal behaviour," and recognizes a distinct category, outside her structural duality, which she calls " 'extranatural' " discourse,

> that is, the production of verbal structures that are not governed by the conventions of either natural *or* fictive discourse: for example, his [the child's] repetition, to no one in particular, of "funny" words, phrases, or phonemes; the semi-melodic and minimally verbal "songs" that he makes up himself; and long streams of essentially private—that is, nonsocial though overt—speech and verbal impersonation.[38]

Herrnstein Smith completes her differentiation of the child's earliest speech by emphasizing that "its forms and occurrences *imperfectly* reflect the conventions of the linguistic community and are *not yet* governed appropriately by the assumptions of natural verbal transactions. It is nonconventional by default not by design."[39] Bissett, I have argued, uses repetition, minimally "verbal" songs, and streams of non-social speech, precisely because the discourse is *extra*natural and not yet governed by the inhibiting conventions of the community. Bissett uses extranatural discourse by design (however much he would pretend it to occur by default); hence, in Herrnstein Smith's terms, it is fictive discourse and poetry, whose essential characteristic is that it demands interpretation by the reader. "I was just cummin," which begins with the speaker's returning from "th vd clinik," and describes people's reactions to a blind man collapsing in the street, is conveyed in bissett's characteristic spelling, and his drifting line, so that we come on the experience, not in shocked anger, but in a kind of vision where all experiences have an equal and interlinked significance. As children join sentences by "and," a "conjunction that does not require specification of the relationship in detail," so bissett ties all his sentences together by and/"nd," suggesting a world of multiple interrelationships, not a world of cause and effect, or of sequence in time.[40]

Even in poems, that is, about Canada, or fucking, or nuclear war, an extranatural discourse, revealed in sound and repetition, in naïve syntax or in overuse of the definite article, will identify the poem with bissett's radically innocent perception of an interdependent and interconnected world. The speaker is always the artist as only child, playing with his language at a stage before meaning, or beyond meaning, where Lee and bissett unite in a self-referential autistic vision. Neither poet is profoundly intellectual, or philosophical: neither poet repays the exploration of meaning, at least in the conventional sense of explicating the types of ambiguity. What their poems invite perhaps is a reading, as intent a reading as possible, of their surface. Like the child's word play, they are poems which begin and end in a self-contained world of language. Or, perhaps, we had better say, they are poems that begin and end before language, and carry us to the magic of surface, to the pleasure of what is there, in sound and repetition, in echoes of child language, rather than in conventional significances.

On Fringe, Cracked Sky, and the Song of Birds

In summer the sun ascends from the sea,
a silent verb of morning, and the song of birds
sits on your tongue: "Why is tomorrow, tomorrow?"
Or, "When I grow up, do you grow down?"
Ron Smith, "Nicole: August 20"

When Ron Smith writes a sonnet sequence in dialogue with the phrases spoken by his five-year-old daughter, he also joins a dialogue with the silent verbs of centuries of lyrics. The poet listens to the child's questions: in the first she tries consciously to manipulate the language's possibilities into understanding, in the other she voices unintentionally one of language's infinite variations that may never have been spoken before. Most adults, and certainly every parent, will remember a surprise of understanding expressed in a child's efforts to comprehend through language.

Marc and Liane, to whom this book is too cryptically dedicated, were learning one, and then a second, and then a third language while this book was being written. I remember Marc, when he had just turned four, waking in the middle of a stormy prairie night to exclaim, "the sky cracked." The remark set me wondering whether we could distinguish a "natural metaphor" so obvious it didn't have to be learned. And now that I know a little about spontaneous metaphor and a child's literalism, I still like the mystery of that phrase that seemed commonplace and novel at the same time. At approximately the same age, Liane asked me one afternoon what was for dessert. "It's in the fridge," Treva told her, having not quite heard the question. The puzzle was solved when at the end of dinner a bowl of sliced oranges and bananas appeared. "Ah, fringe," said Liane enthusiastically. Ever since, we've thought of oranges and bananas as our fringe dessert, somehow slightly frayed and borderline, to be eaten when something sweeter, or creamier, or cakier cannot be found.

More recently I heard a CBC Radio program about the impact of the rock video. In summary one commentator enthusiastically quoted his seven-year-old daughter: "Daddy, Daddy, they're playing videos on the radio." Here the child's comment reveals a cultural shift more fully, more persuasively, than we had dared, or bothered, to think. And while I'm on the subject of television, top ratings for "The Cosby Show" may have had something to do with Bill Cosby's being far and away the best comedian of the child's point of view. When Cosby reproduces children's voices, we recognize the rigidity of playground morality: "You can't hit another kid with a slush ball!"

From the family dinner table to the TV screen, child language surrounds us. If this book could convey, in a few of its moments, the way in which that language can shape a poem, including the poetry of the novel, and the story, and the stage, I would be satisfied. In dealing with a subject so universally familiar, and an academic discipline which was completely new to me, I have been continually aware, especially in the last rewriting of the manuscript, of the angles and byways and interstices still to be explored. If some sense of the unfinished, the untested, and the mistaken adheres to the book, then it is at least appropriate to the way we grow down on the way to growing up.

BIBLIOGRAPHICAL NOTES

Since the range of sources upon which this book is based is fairly comprehensively represented in my endnotes, I have not attached a separate bibliography. The following note focuses on ancillary reading.

That central Canadian poem, F. R. Scott's "Laurentian Shield," comes to a curious ending with the prediction (?) that we "can turn this rock into children" (*An Anthology of Canadian Literature*, Russell Brown and Donna Bennett eds. [Toronto: Oxford Univ. Press, 1982], I, p. 353). Although the poem begins in "wonder" and ponders the connections between language and comprehension, this final metaphor remains, for me, perplexing. The writing of this book has prompted me to ask the question again, but it has not resolved the perplexity. Scott's poem might function, then, as a reminder of the pervasiveness of the image of the child in literature, and of its inherent mystery. Certainly a study of the *image* of childhood in Canadian literature could be massive, ranging from Charles G.D. Roberts's inescapable celebration of the "Child of Nations, giant-limbed" ("Canada," *100 Poems of Nineteenth Century Canada*, Douglas Lochhead and Raymond Souster, eds. [Toronto: Macmillan, 1974], pp. 113-14) to five-year-old Isobel at the opening of Audrey Thomas's *Songs My Mother Taught Me* (Vancouver: Talonbooks, 1973), from Charles Heavysege's sonnet, "Childhood alone is glad" ("Sonnet Sequence from *Jephthah's Daughter*," *100 Poems of Nineteenth Century Canada*, p. 7) to Margaret Atwood's movingly reverent admonition to her daughter in "You Begin" (*Two-Headed Poems* [Toronto: Oxford, 1978], pp. 110-11). I did not write this sort of study and have avoided drawing conclusions about a peculiarly Canadian dimension of the topic.

Those interested in reading further about the figure of the child in Canadian literature will find direction to the most appropriate titles and writers in such teachers' handbooks as M.G. Hesse, ed., *Childhood and Youth in Canadian Literature* (Toronto: Macmillan, 1979), *Coming of Age in Canada*, British Columbia Work Group, Andreas Schroeder et al., comps. (Toronto: The Writers' Development Trust, n.d.), Don Gutteridge, *Rites of Passage* (Toronto: McClelland & Stewart, 1979), and Elizabeth Waterston, *Survey: A Short History of Canadian Literature* (Toronto:

Methuen, 1973), pp. 147-51, 157-58. The most extended studies of the subject are Margery Fee, "Romantic Nationalism and the Child in Canadian Writing," *Canadian Children's Literature* 18-19 (1980): 46-61, and Thomas Tausky, " 'A Passion to Live in this Splendid Past': Canadian and Australian Autobiographies of Childhood," *Ariel*, 17:3 (July 1986): 39-62. Eli Mandel makes a number of comments about the pastoral and the child in "The Study of Canadian Culture," *English Quarterly* 4: 3 (Fall 1971): 20. See also his remarks on the child figure in regional literature, "Images of Prairie Man," in *Another Time* (Erin, Ont.: Press Porcepic, 1977), pp. 49-51. For a sense of child innocence in its wider mythological context, see D.G. Jones "In Search of America," *Boundary II* 3: 1 (Fall 1974): 227-46.

Literature written in French in Canada is perhaps even more attached to the child figure than literature in English. The best general introduction of the source material is Denise Lemieux, *Une Culture de la nostalgie: L'enfant dans le roman québécois de ses origines à nos jours* (Montreal: Boréal Express, 1984). Since the book is a survey by sociologists, it makes almost no comment on style or language, but as a study of how changes in the image of the child in fiction reflect cultural changes in Québec, it is quite extensive.

Of general studies of the image of childhood in literature Richard Coe's *When the Grass Was Taller: Autobiography and the Experience of Childhood* (New Haven and London: Yale Univ. Press, 1984) is of special interest because it incorporates both French-Canadian and English-Canadian autobiographies in discussion of a genre which also includes American, British, French, Russian, African, and Australian examples. I read Coe's book while I was making final revisions to this book; therefore, my few references to it may not suggest how strongly I recommend the book as a companion study to my own. The closest Coe comes to my specific subject is in a passing reference to an alternative dimension implicit in child language, in its "malapropisms and misunderstandings, its inappropriate cross-references effected in the subconscious, its voluntary puns with their involuntary but revealing symbolism" (pp. 265-66). But he is continuously interesting in his more general discussion of the problems which face writers who set out to describe their childhood, and he gives a valuable sense of the history of the forms and styles which lie behind my topic. The other invaluable text on the figure of the child in English literature is Peter Coveney's *The Image of Childhood: The Individual and Society: A Study of the Theme in English Literature,* rev. ed. (1957; rpt. Harmondsworth, Eng.: Penguin, 1967), a book which continues to be an excellent source of ideas for anyone interested in the child in literature. Two more general studies, which incline, in this order, toward a history-of-ideas approach are Reinhard Kuhn's *Corruption in Paradise: The Child in Western Literature* (Hanover,

NH: Univ. Press of New England, 1982), and Robert Pattison, *The Child Figure in English Literature* (Athens: Univ. of Georgia Press, 1978). A more idiosyncratic book in this genre, interesting for its unusual comparative study of writers separated by three centuries, is Michael Long's *Marvell, Nabokov: Childhood and Arcadia* (Oxford: Clarendon Press, 1984). Among many other less closely related studies I would particularly recommend for limpid and stimulating readability: Tony Tanner's *The Reign of Wonder: Naivety and Reality in American Literature* (Cambridge, Eng.: Cambridge Univ. Press, 1965), and Fernando Savater, *Childhood Regained: The Art of the Storyteller*, trans. Frances M. Lopez-Morillas (Irvington, NY: Columbia Univ. Press, 1982). Two excellent articles came to my attention after the manuscript was at the copy-editing stage: Naomi B. Sokoloff's "Interpretation: Cynthia Ozick's *Cannibal* Galaxy," *Prooftexts* 6 (1986): 239-57 connects semiotics to social implications in a study of the depiction of children; Brian McHale's "Speaking as a Child in *U.S.A.*: A Problem in the Mimesis of Speech," *Language and Style* 17:4 (Fall 1984): 351-70, outlines very succinctly the theoretical problems involved specifically in representing child speech, and presents a point-by-point outline of the usual linguistic signals of child language.

Mary Jane Hurst's thesis "The Voice of the Child in American Literature: Linguistic Approaches to Fictional Child Language" (Ph.D Maryland 1986) emphasizes literary representations of children's speech.

NOTES

PREFACE: INTERSECTIONS IN
SURPRISE

1. Robert Kroetsch, "back in the spring of '76: for Laurie Ricou," *Advice to My* *Friends: A Continuing Poem* (Don Mills, Ont.: Stoddart, 1985), p. 18.

CHAPTER ONE: THE "AS IF" OF THE
CHILD'S WORLD

Epigraphs: James E. Miller, Jr., *Word, Self, Reality: The Rhetoric of Imagination* (New York: Dodd Mead, 1973), p. 150; Theodore Roethke, "Open Letter," in *Mid-century American Poets*, ed. John Ciardi (New York: Twayne, 1950), p. 70; Breyne Arlene Moskowitz, "The Acquisition of Language," *Scientific American* (November 1978): 92.

1. Noam Chomsky's linguistic theories of the 1950s promoted a massive (and still expanding) increase in studies of child language. See Adele A. Abrahamsen, *Child Language: An Interdisciplinary Guide to Theory and Research* (Baltimore: Univ. Park Press, 1977) and the annual bibliographies *Child Development Abstracts and Bibliography* (Univ. of Chicago Press) and *Language and Language Behavior Abstracts* (Univ. of Michigan).
2. Roethke, "Open Letter," p. 70.
3. *Ibid.*, p. 68.
4. Roethke, *The Collected Poems*, Anchor Books Edition (Garden City, NY: Doubleday, 1975), pp. 50-52. *The Lost Son and Other Poems* was first published in 1948.
5. See e.g., M. Bowerman, *Early Syntactic Development* (Cambridge: Cambridge Univ. Press, 1973); B. L. Derwing, *Transformational Grammar as a Theory of Language* (Cambridge, MA: Harvard Univ. Press, 1973).
6. Peter A. and Jill G. de Villiers, *Early Language* (Cambridge, Mass.: Harvard

Univ. Press, 1979), p. 84-89.
7. It's no surprise, for example, that the calling card for *Resounding*, the sound poetry duet of Douglas Barbour and Stephen Scobie, proudly carries a one-word excerpt from a *New York Times* review: "infantile." As Scobie rationalized the criticism: " 'Infant' derives from the Latin negative prefix *in*-and *fans*, present participle of *fare*—to speak. An infant is one who is 'not speaking' who has not yet evolved the ability to articulate ideas into words. So 'infantile' means 'pre-linguistic,' prior to speech, down there in the ol' primeval swamp of sound." Scobie, "In the City at the End of Things," *NeWest ReView* (May, 1980), pp. 14-15.
8. Moskowitz, 'The Acquisition of Language,' p. 96.
9. *Ibid.* I have simplified Moskowitz's example.
10. *Ibid.*
11. *Ibid.*, p. 98.
12. *Ibid.*, p. 95.
13. de Villiers, *Early Language*, p. 31.
14. *Ibid.*, pp. 46-47.
15. *Ibid.*, p. 37.
16. Moskowitz, "The Acquisition of Language," p. 106.
17. *Ibid.* p. 98.
18. de Villiers, *Early Language*, p. 36. For an introduction to the literature on the subject see, for example, Howard Pollio, Jack Barlow, Harold Fine, and Marilyn

Pollio, *Psychology and the Poetics of Growth: Figurative Language in Psychology, Psychotherapy, and Education* (Hillsdale, NJ: Lawrence Erlbaum, 1977); Andrew Ortony, Ralph Reynolds, and Judith Arter, "Metaphor: Theoretical and Empirical Research," *Psychological Bulletin* 85:5 (September 1978): 919-43; Andrew Ortony, ed., *Metaphor and Thought* (Cambridge, Eng.: Cambridge Univ. Press, 1979); Richard M. Billow, "Observing Spontaneous Metaphor in Children," *Journal of Experimental Child Psychology* 31 (1981): 430-45.

19. See my Bibliographical Notes in this volume.

20. Robert Scholes, *Structuralism in Literature: An Introduction* (New Haven, CT: Yale Univ. Press, 1974), p. 19.

21. *Ibid.*, p. 20. See Roman Jakobson and Moms Halle, "The Metaphoric and Metonymic Poles," *Fundamentals of Language* (The Hague: Mouton, 1956), pp. 76-82.

22. Sister A. Martha Westwater suggests that *Alice in Wonderland* is the first important expression of this aspect of the child's mind in fiction. "Towards Understanding Coincidence in Children's Literature," *Canadian Children's Literature* 5/6 (1976): 19.

23. In connecting Dickens's "reverence for childhood" with his "literary genius," Angus Wilson emphasizes several themes and attitudes:

> deep concern with inanimate objects and their endowment with an autonomous life which is yet sympathetic to the human life lived out among them; fascination with dreaming and half-waking states; belief in meaningful legendary shapes informing everyday real life; a sense of absurdity poised delicately between cruelty and compassion; the forms and the language of memory and the tricks that it plays upon time, places and persons.

But Wilson says little about psychology or fictional technique and nothing about their intersection. "Dickens on Children and Childhood," in *Dickens 1970: Centenary Essays*, ed. Michael Slater (London: Chapman and Hall, 1970), p. 201. Despite the obvious potential, few critics have

made extended connection between Dickens's language and the child's perspective. Norman Page, for example, in his chapter "Dickens and Speech," discusses repetition and disappearance of the sentence but does not connect these to child language; see his *Speech in the English Novel* (London: Longman, 1973), 133-60. Many studies of the figure of the child, like Wilson's, obliquely suggest possible approaches. See, for example, comments on caricature and the "child's-eye view" in Jacqueline P. Banerjee, "Ambivalence and Contradictions: The Child in Victorian Fiction," *English Studies* 65: 6 (1984): 481-94.

24. Muriel G. Shine, *The Fictional Children of Henry James* (Chapel Hill: Univ. of North Carolina Press, 1968), p. 172.

25. Richard N. Coe, *When the Grass Was Taller: Autobiography and the Experience of Childhood* (New Haven, Conn.: Yale Univ. Press, 1984), p. 83.

26. Coe, *When the Grass Was Taller*, p. 253.

27. *Ibid.*

28. James Joyce, *A Portrait of the Artist as a Young Man* (1916; rpt. New York: Viking, 1964), p. 12. Remarking on how the last two sentences of this passage give meaning to the earlier infant song "O, the green wothe botheth," Richard Coe comments: "The trouble is that this is all too neat; *everything* fits in, everything is part of a pattern. There are no trivialities in Joyce, any more than there are in Proust." *When the Grass Was Taller*, p. 213; cf. his other comments on the novel, pp. 83-84.

29. Joyce, *A Portrait*, p. 70.

30. Readers probably first think of successful writing about children as language which gives the illusion of an exclusively sensory perception. In discussing "The Imagery of Childhood in Nathalie Sarraute's *Portrait d'un inconnu*," Valerie Minogue describes the child narrator's language as "a language barely separable from sensation, an imagery drawn from our first experience of the world, from physical pleasure or disgust, or recollections of childish games." *French Studies* 27 (1973): 179. Cf. "The magic objects of childhood (and this *is* their magic) communicate directly, without the intermediate stage of rational conceptualization." Coe,

When the Grass Was Taller, p. 260.

31. Peter Coveney, *The Image of Childhood: The Individual and Society: A Study of the Theme in English Literature*, rev. ed. (1957; rpt. Harmondsworth, Eng.: Penguin Books, 1967), p. 318.

32. bill bissett, *Selected Poems: Beyond Even Faithful Legends* (Vancouver: Talonbooks, 1980), p. 21.

33. de Villiers, *Early Language*, p. 89.

34. bissett, "beyond even faithful legends,"

in *Selected Poems*, p. 28.

35. In this context the question might arise as to whether psycholinguists have found literature to be a good source. I have found only the two cited in Alison J. Elliot, *Child Language* (Cambridge, Eng.: Cambridge Univ. Press, 1981), 160.

36. Tom Robbins, *Even Cowgirls Get the Blues* (1976; rpt. New York: Bantam, 1977), p. 16.

CHAPTER TWO: THE LANGUAGE OF CHILDHOOD REMEMBERED

Epigraphs: Alice Munro, "Tell Me Yes or No," *Something I've Been Meaning to Tell You: Thirteen Stories*, Signet Edition (1974; rpt. Scarborough, Ont.: New American Library, 1975), p. 86; Margaret Laurence, "Where the World Began," *Heart of a Stranger*, Seal Books Edition (1976; rpt. Toronto: McClelland & Stewart-Bantam, 1980), p. 242 (originally published in *Maclean's*, December 1972).

1. Margaret Laurence, *A Bird in the House*, Seal Books Edition (1970; rpt. Toronto: McClelland & Stewart-Bantam, 1978), pp. 13-14. Further references to the novel are identified by the abbreviation *BH* in parentheses.

2. Alice Munro, *Lives of Girls and Women*, Signet Edition (1971; rpt. Scarborough, Ont.: New American Library, 1974), p. 45. Further references to the novel are identified by the abbreviation *LGW* in parentheses.

3. Leona Gom, "Laurence and the Use of Memory," *Canadian Literature* 71 (Winter 1976): 54, 55.

4. Helen Hoy, letter to the author, 21 July, 1983.

5. Ronald N. Labonté, "Disclosing and Touching: Revaluating the Manawaka World," *Journal of Canadian Fiction* 27 (1980): 173, 172.

6. Leslie Fiedler, "The Eye of Innocence," *No! in Thunder: Essays on Myth and Literature* (Boston: Beacon Press, 1960), pp. 280-81.

7. In *Dreams of Speech and Violence: The Art of the Short Story in Canada and New Zealand* (Toronto: Univ. of Toronto Press, 1987), pp. 187-200. W. H. New shows that the child's acceptance of

"disorder" is one aspect of the young Vanessa that the adult narrator grows to recognize.

8. Marcel Proust, *Remembrance of Things Past*, I, trans. C.K. Scott Moncrieff and Terence Kilmartin, Vintage Books Edition (New York: Random House, 1982), p. 48.

9. Kent Thompson notes that the usual modern short story form, with its crucial "epiphany," is not characteristic of these stories. See his review of *A Bird in the House*, *Fiddlehead* 84 (1970): 108-11, rpt. in W.H. New, ed., *Margaret Laurence* (Toronto: McGraw-Hill Ryerson, 1977), p. 153.

10. Jerome Buckley, *Season of Youth: The Bildungsroman from Dickens to Golding* (Cambridge, MA: Harvard Univ. Press, 1974), p. 17-18. Also relevant to this discussion are Rosalie Murphy Baum, "Artist and Woman: Young Lives in Laurence and Munro," *North Dakota Quarterly* 52: 3 (Summer 1984): 196-211, and Margaret K. Butcher, "From *Maurice Guest* to *Martha Quest*: The Female Bildungsroman in Commonwealth Literature," *WLWE* 21: 2 (Summer 1982): 254-62. Cf. W.R. Martin, "The Strange and the Familiar in Alice Munro," *Studies in Canadian Literature* 7: 2 (1982): 214-26, which links Del's growth to the growth of the foetus and the stages of evolution.

11. Anthony B. Dawson, "Coming of Age in Canada," *Mosaic* 11:3 (Spring 1978): 47.

12. Roger Fowler, *Linguistics and the Novel* (London: Methuen, 1977), p. 116.

13. Labonté, "Disclosing and Touching," p. 172.

146 NOTES

14. Fowler, *Linguistics and the Novel*, p. 102.
15. Simone Vauthier, "Notes on the Narrative Voice(s) in *The Stone Angel*," *Etudes Canadiennes/Canadian Studies* 11(décembre 1981): 131-53. Vauthier distinguishes the narrator, who is *"telling"* her story," from the *locutor*, who is *"living* what the reader apprehends as her story" (p. 133).
16. Carole Peterson and Alyssa McCabe, *Developmental Psycholinguistics: Three Ways of Looking at a Child's Narratives* (New York: Plenum Press, 1983), pp. 59, 85.
17. Helen Hoy, " 'Dull, Simple, Amazing and Unfathomable': Paradox and Double Vision in Alice Munro's Fiction," *Studies in Canadian Literature*, 5:1 (Spring 1980): 100, 103, 104.

18. Joseph Church, *Language and the Discovery of Reality* (New York: Random House, 1961), p. 66.
19. See Robert G. Malgady, "Children's Interpretation and Appreciation of Similes," *Child Development* 48:4 (1977): 1734-38.
20. Fowler, *Linguistics and the Novel*, p. 119.
21. *Ibid.*, p. 126.
22. Excerpts of several of Laurence's works have been performed on stage by Norma Edwards, in her own adaptation titled *The Women of Margaret Laurence*. For some implications of the stage metaphor and its connection to adolescence persisting, see Susan J. Warwick, "Growing Up: The Novels of Alice Munro," *Essays on Canadian Writing* 29 (Summer 1984): 204-25.

CHAPTER THREE: A RHETORIC OF BEGINNINGS

Epigraphs: The epigraph from Jean-Paul Sartre is cited in Clark Blaise, *A North American Education: A Book of Short Fiction* (1973; rpt. Don Mills, Ont.: General, 1974), p. 131. Further references to this work are identified by the abbreviation *NAE* in parentheses. The second epigraph is from Clark Blaise and Bharati Mukherjee, *Days and Nights in Calcutta* (Garden City, NY: Doubleday, 1977), p. 7.

1. Alfred Kazin, "A Procession of Children," *American Scholar* 33 (Spring 1964): 182.
2. Peter Coveney, *The Image of Childhood*, rev. ed. (1957; rpt. Harmondsworth, Eng.: Penguin Books, 1967), p. 195.
3. Clark Blaise, *Tribal Justice* (1974; rpt. Don Mills, Ont.: General, 1975), p. 60. Further references are identified by the abbreviation *TJ* in parentheses.
4. William Carlos Williams, "The Descent," *Selected Poems of William Carlos Williams* (New York: New Directions, 1968), p. 132.
5. Frederick Elkin, *The Child and Society: The Process of Socialization* (1960; rpt. New York: Random House, 1966), pp. 63-65.
6. Erik H. Erikson, *Childhood and Society*, 2nd ed. (1950; rpt. New York: W.W. Norton, 1963), p. 216.

7. Frank Davey, "Impressionable Realism: The Stories of Clark Blaise," *Open Letter*, 3rd ser., No. 5 (Summer 1976): 70.
8. Clark Blaise, "To Begin, To Begin," in John Metcalf, ed., *The Narrative Voice: Short Stories and Reflections by Canadian Authors* (Toronto: McGraw-Hill Ryerson, 1972), pp. 23-24.
9. The other "Thibidault stories" give different biographies for Frankie: another pattern of rebeginnings.
10. Blaise, "To Begin, To Begin," p. 22.
11. Davey, "Impressionable Realism," p. 68.
12. Robert Lecker, "Clark Blaise: Murals Deep in Nature," in *On the Line: Readings in the Short Fiction of Clark Blaise, John Metcalf, and Hugh Hood* (Downsview, Ont.: ECW Press, 1982), p. 42. This briskly written study of the "confrontation between sensibility and . . . inexplicable ugliness" (p. 28) in Blaise's art frequently, in its focus on "rawness," comments on the ideas in this chapter. Particularly relevant are Lecker's comments on the "perpetual traveller" (p. 29), on the uncertainty of learning language (p. 20), on "A North American Education" as a "story about starting points" (p. 33), and especially on the form of pre-story: "To make *notes* is to pursue the story before the story, the mysterious entrance to the past which remains fiction, remains art" (p. 52).

CHAPTER FOUR: STAGES OF
LANGUAGE AND LEARNING

Epigraph: Richard N. Coe, *When the Grass Was Taller: Autobiography and the Experience of Childhood* (New Haven, CT: Yale Univ. Press, 1984), p. 130.

1. Ernest Buckler, *Ox Bells and Fireflies* (1968; rpt. Toronto: McClelland & Stewart, 1974), p. 74.
2. Buckler, *Ox Bells and Fireflies*, p. 3.
3. Alfred Kazin, "A Procession of Children," *The American Scholar* 33 (Spring 1964): 177.
4. W.O. Mitchell, *Who Has Seen the Wind* (1947; rpt. Toronto: Macmillan, 1966): p. 4. Subsequent quotations from the novel are identified by page number in parentheses.
5. Joseph Church, *Language and the Discovery of Reality* (New York: Random House, 1961), pp. 96, 98.
6. Jean Piaget, *The Language and Thought of the Child,* 2nd ed. (1926; rpt. London: Routledge, 1932), p. 38. After publication of an earlier version of this chapter in *Canadian Children's Literature* 10 (1977-78): 3-17, I learned that Mitchell was studying Piaget just before writing *Who Has Seen the Wind*. See Michael Peterman, " 'The Good Game': The Charm of Willa Cather's *My Antonia* and W.O. Mitchell's *Who Has Seen the Wind*," *Mosaic* 14:2 (Spring 1981): 97.
7. Piaget, *The Language and Thought of the Child*, 14.
8. J. Huizinga, *Homo Ludens: A Study of the Play-Element in Culture* (1950; rpt. Boston: Beacon Press, 1955), p. 119.
9. The psychologists' term for this mental process is transductive reasoning. For a reading of the novel as poetry, see S.A. Gingell-Beckmann, "The Lyricism of W.O. Mitchell's *Who Has Seen the Wind*," *Studies in Canadian Literature* 6:2 (1981): 221-31.
10. The years from seven to eleven or twelve are known as the period of "concrete operations." For a useful condensation of Piaget's theory of the stages in the development of thought see Jean Piaget, *The Psychology of Intelligence* (1947; rpt.

London: Routledge, 1950), p. 123. Of course, almost all introductory psychology texts will also provide an outline of Piaget's scheme. See, for example, Guy R. Lefrancois, *Of Children: An Introduction to Child Development* (Belmont, CA: Wadsworth, 1973), p. 156.
11. For an outline of Kohlberg's levels and types of morality see Lefrancois, *Of Children*, p. 301.
12. Piaget, *The Language and Thought of the Child*, p. 166.
13. I am using the terms "metaphor" and "simile" interchangeably, leaving until Chapter 5 discussion of the idea that the simile seems more congenial to the child since it makes the link more visible, more grammatically available.
14. Huizinga, *Homo Ludens*, p. 17.
15. C.G. Jung, "The Phenomenology of the Spirit in Fairy Tales," *Psyche and Symbol: A Selection from the Writings of C.G. Jung*, ed. Violet S. de Laszlo, Anchor Books ed. (Garden City: Doubleday, 1958), p. 65.
16. There may be some connection between Brian's cursing and the behaviour described in William Labov's influential study, "Rules for Ritual Insults," *Studies in Social Interaction*, ed. David Sudnow (New York: Free Press, 1972), pp. 120-69. "By social convention it is accepted that they [ritual insults] do not denote attributes that persons actually possess." They provide, Labov explains, "sanctuar[y]" and a context in which the speaker is "freed from personal responsibility." p. 168.
17. Mark Twain, *The Adventures of Tom Sawyer*, (New York: Harper & Row, 1965), p. 208.
18. William Wordsworth, "Ode: Intimations of Immortality from Recollections of Early Childhood," ll. 142-53.
19. Jerome Hamilton Buckley, *Season of Youth: The Bildungsroman from Dickens to Golding* (Cambridge, MA: Harvard Univ. Press, 1974), p. 4.

148 NOTES

CHAPTER FIVE: DELIGHT WITHOUT
JUDGEMENT

Quotations from unpublished material by kind permission of the late Mr. Ernest Buckler.
Epigraph: Carl Gustav Jung, "The Phenomenology of the Spirit in Fairy-tales," *The Archetypes and the Collective Unconscious,* trans. R.F.C. Hull, 2nd ed., Vol. IX of *Collected Works.* (London: Routledge & Kegan Paul, 1969), pp. 223-24.

1. Ernest Buckler, *The Mountain and the Valley* (1952; rpt. Toronto: McClelland & Stewart, 1961), p. 296. Page references throughout refer to this edition.
2. Claude Bissell, "Introduction," *The Mountain and the Valley,* (1961), p. x.
3. Emily M. Beck, Trade Editorial Report on "The Mountain and the Valley," Atlantic Monthly Press, 25 April, 1951, Box 15, Ernest Buckler Collection, Univ. of Toronto Library.
4. Alan Young, *Ernest Buckler,* Canadian Writers Series No. 15 (Toronto: McClelland & Stewart, 1976), p. 17.
5. Ernest Buckler to Dudley Cloud, Atlantic Monthly Press, 15 May, 1951, Box 15, Ernest Buckler Collection.
6. A.O.J. Cockshut, in *The Art of Autobiography in 19th and 20th Century England* (New Haven, CT: Yale Univ. Press, 1984) observes how the genre (unlike biography) emphasizes the importance of childhood. It is tempting, given this perspective, to define *The Mountain and the Valley* as fictional autobiography, rather than *Künstlerroman.*
7. Cf. Dave Godfrey's review of *The Cruelest Month,* "Buckler and Allen," *Tamarack Review* 36 (Summer 1965): 83.
8. Draft No. 1, "The Mountain and the Valley," Box 13, and Draft No. 2, "The Mountain and the Valley," Box 14, Ernest Buckler Collection.
9. M.D. Vernon, *The Psychology of Perception,* 2nd ed. (Harmondsworth, Eng.: Penguin Books, 1971), p. 86.
10. Frank Davey and bpNichol, "Notions of Image," *Open Letter,* Series 5, No. 7 (Spring 1984): 80, 77. This article provides a clear summary of the literary

applications of simile (as differentiated from metaphor).
11. Draft No. 1, "The Mountain and the Valley," Box 13, Ernest Buckler Collection.
12. Vernon, *Psychology of Perception,* p. 78.
13. Presumably this is another dilemma which Buckler shares with David. Consider Buckler's admiration for Hemingway: "I think that all writers should be locked up for several weeks inside a sonnet with no food but Hemingway, so that they could at least learn the discipline of the tight line before they flout it," *Esquire,* February 1973, p. 6. Quoted in Young, *Ernest Buckler,* p. 20.
14. William Empson, *Some Versions of Pastoral* (London: Chatto and Windus, 1968), p. 261.
15. Warren Tallman, "Wolf in the Snow," *Canadian Literature* 5 (Summer 1960): 13.
16. Alan Young suggests the necessity of taking a more ironic view of David, and provides one context for such reassessment, in *Ernest Buckler,* pp. 36-37.
17. Draft No. 1, Box 13, Ernest Buckler Collection.
18. Maurice Merleau-Ponty, "The Child's Relations with Others," *The Primacy of Perception and Other Essays on Phenomenological Psychology, the Philosophy of Art, History and Politics,* ed. James M. Edie (Evanston, IL: Northwestern Univ. Press, 1964), p. 150.
19. William S. Rubin, *Dada and Surrealist Art* (New York: Harry N. Abrams, 1968), p. 22. To extend the exploration of literary cubism (its mathematical forms and deliberate ambiguity) in Buckler, one might begin with the possibilities implicit in Jack F. Stewart, "Cubist Elements in *Between the Acts,*" *Mosaic* 18:2 (Spring 1985): 65-89.
20. William S. Rubin, *Dada and Surrealist Art,* p. 23.
21. X.J. Kennedy, "Nude Descending a Staircase," *Poems, Songs/A Ballad* (Garden City, NJ: Doubleday, 1961), p. 69.

CHAPTER SIX: EMILY CARR AND
THE LANGUAGE OF SMALL

Epigraph: Margaret Atwood, *Surfacing* (Toronto: McClelland & Stewart 1972), p. 181.

1. Emily Carr, *The Book of Small* (1942; rpt. Toronto: Clarke Irwin, 1966), p. 15. Subsequent references are identified in parentheses.
2. Mary Louise Craven, "Emily Carr," *Profiles in Canadian Literature Series I*, ed. Jeffrey M. Heath (Toronto: Dundurn Press, 1980), p. 57.
3. Emily Carr, *Hundreds and Thousands: The Journals of Emily Carr* (Toronto: Clarke Irwin, 1966), pp. 98-99.
4. Roger Fowler, *Linguistics and the Novel* (London: Methuen, 1977), p. 102.
5. Emily Carr, *Klee Wyck* (1941; rpt. Toronto: Clarke Irwin, 1971), p. 18.
6. Emily Carr, *Fresh Seeing* (Toronto: Clarke Irwin, 1972), p. 8. Paul Klee's enthusiasm for the child's perspective seems a strong influence here. A sense of the parallels between Klee's writing and painting and Carr's, is provoked, for example, by James Smith Pierce, *Paul Klee and Primitive Art* (New York: Garland, 1976).
7. The ordering of pieces under a single title may not be all Carr's doing. I follow the Clarke Irwin versions, which remain in print. But clearly study of the manuscripts and provenance of the sketches must follow before we can draw definitive conclusions. That one of the most popular children's books of the twentieth century, A.A. Milne's *Winnie the Pooh* (1926), also uses the name seems to corroborate its appropriateness. But I know of no evidence that Carr knew the book.
8. Peter A. and Jill G. de Villiers, *Early Language* (Cambridge, MA: Harvard Univ. Press, 1979), pp. 68-70. It may also be relevant that children seem to use articles to differentiate the imaginary play world ("*the* mummy" to designate a doll) from the actual world ("*mummy*") in the same discourse. "Small" seems to insist

on a unique individual in the actual world. See Sven Strömquist, "Remarks on Referential Ambiguity in Play," *Gothenburg Papers in Theoretical Linguistics* 43 (Göteborg, Sweden: Univ. of Gothenburg, Department of Linguistics, 1981).
9. See, for example, Anne Sinclair, "Thinking about Language: An Interview Study of Children Aged Three to Eight," *International Journal of Psycholinguistics* 7:4 (1980).
10. Carr, *Hundreds and Thousands*, p. 311.
11. Among students of child language there is some disagreement on this point. See Alison J. Elliot, *Child Language* (Cambridge, Eng.: Cambridge Univ. Press, 1981), p. 83; and Breyne Arlene Moskowitz, "The Acquisition of Language," *Scientific American* (November 1978): 95.
12. de Villiers, *Child Language*, p. 46.
13. Carr, *Klee Wyck*, p. 79.
14. For the distinction between "active metaphor" and "copula metaphor" see Frank Davey and bp Nichol, "Notions of Image," *Open Letter*, Series 5, No. 7 (Spring 1984): pp. 79-80. Their compact epigraph, NOUNS VERB/THINGS DO, could be taken as the fundamental principle of Carr's prose.
15. de Villiers, *Child Language*, p. 35.
16. Ira Dilworth, "Foreword," *Klee Wyck*, unpaginated.
17. Elliot, *Child Language*, p. 151. The overuse of proper names in caretaker language would imply, in this context, Carr approaching her own character as a mother would a child.
18. Joseph Church, *Language and the Discovery of Reality* (New York: Random House, 1961), p. 73.
19. Elliot, *Child Language*, p. 58.
20. E.L. Epstein, *Language and Style* (London: Methuen, 1978), p. 14.
21. Florence McNeil, "Being a Writer," "To the Ladies of the Art Society," *Emily* (Toronto: Clarke Irwin, 1975), pp. 62, 34.

CHAPTER SEVEN: INFANT
SENSIBILITY AND LYRIC STRATEGY

Epigraphs: Kornei Chukovsky, *From Two to Five*, trans. and ed. Miriam Morton. Rev. ed. (1925; trans. Berkeley: Univ. of California Press, 1968), pp. 2-3; Dylan Thomas, "Poem in October," *The Collected Poems of Dylan Thomas 1934-1952* (rev. 1956; rpt. New York: New Directions, 1971) p. 115.

1. Some survey of the child and the romantic lyric is found in Coveney, *Image of Childhood*, especially the chapters on Blake, and Wordworth and Coleridge, pp. 52-90. Coe's *When the Grass Was Taller* concerns the poet and child throughout; his discussion of Thomas Traherne as a predecessor is valuable as a further example, pp. 25-27, 254-58.

2. Cf. Winifred Nowottny, *The Language Poets Use* (1962; rpt. London: Athlone, 1965), for the argument that Dylan Thomas's language should be interpreted as "the language of a child": "The child uses the phrase that seems to him to be the most direct and accurate description of what he is talking about, but because adult conventions of meaning demand that we say what we mean in the way other people would say it, the child's description strikes us, not as factual, but as quaint or even incomprehensible" (p. 195). See also Diane Wood Middlebrook, "Summoning Childhood: Poetry of Dylan Thomas," in her *Worlds into Words: Understanding Modern Poems* (New York: Norton, 1978), pp. 23-45.

3. A.M. Klein, "Portrait of the Poet as Landscape," *The Collected Poems of A.M. Klein*, comp. Miriam Waddington (Toronto: McGraw-Hill Ryerson, 1974), 330-35.

4. W.B. Carnochan "The Child Is Father of the Man" in Patricia Meyer Spacks and W.B. Carnochan, *A Distant Prospect: Eighteenth-Century Views of Childhood* (Los Angeles: William Andrews Clark Memorial Library, Univ. of California, 1982), pp. 30, 34-35, 42.

5. P.K. Page, "The Snowman," *Cry Ararat! Poems New and Selected* (Toronto: McClelland & Stewart, 1967), p. 32. See Constance Rooke "P.K. Page: The Chameleon and the Centre," *Malahat Review* 45 (Jan. 1978): 169-95. Rooke notes that for Page childhood represents "a preconditioned state of being" and "a period of inchoate dreams." She includes brief discussions of "Stories of Snow" and "Only Child."

6. Page, "Questions and Images," *Canadian Literature* 41 (Summer 1969), 17-18.

7. Page, "Cry Ararat!" *Cry Ararat!*, p. 105.

8. *Ibid.*, p. 106.

9. Page, "Stefan," *Evening Dance of the Grey Flies* (Toronto: Oxford, 1981), p. 21.

10. Page, "Only Child," *Cry Ararat!*, p. 44.

11. Page, "Stories of Snow," *Cry Ararat!*, pp. 26-27.

12. Reinhard Kuhn, *Corruption in Paradise: The Child in Western Literature* (Hanover, NH: Univ. Press of New England, 1982), p. 201.

13. Dorothy Livesay, "Song and Dance," *Canadian Literature* 41 (Summer 1969): 41.

14. Livesay, *Collected Poems: The Two Seasons* (Toronto: McGraw-Hill Ryerson, 1972), p. 52.

15. Livesay, *Collected Poems*, p. 262.

16. Livesay, "On Seeing," *Collected Poems*, p. 216.

17. Livesay, "Perceptions," *Collected Poems*, p. 276.

18. Livesay, *Collected Poems*, p. 162.

19. Livesay, "Growth," *Collected Poems*, p. 22.

20. Livesay, "This Canadian Poetry," *Canadian Forum* (April 1944): 21.

21. Livesay, "The Children's Letters," *Collected Poems*, p. 349.

22. Carnochan, *Distant Prospect*, p. 44.

23. Miriam Waddington, "Things of the World," *Driving Home: Poems New and Selected* (Toronto: Oxford, 1972), p. 115.

24. Waddington, "Portrait: Old Woman" *The Price of Gold* (Toronto: Oxford, 1976), p. 68. For fuller comment on this poem, and on Waddington's imagery see my article, "Into My Green World: The Poetry of Miriam Waddington," *Essays on Canadian Writing* 12 (Fall 1978): 144-61.

25. Waddington, "Snow Stories," *Price of Gold*, p. 45.

26. Waddington, "Artists and Old Chairs,"

"Popular Geography," *Price of Gold*, pp. 82-84, 75.

27. Waddington, "Husbands," *Price of Gold*, p. 57.

28. Waddington, "Laughter," *Driving Home*, p. 84.

29. Chukovsky, *From Two to Five*, pp. 63-79.

30. Robin Skelton, "The Calligraphy Lesson," *Limits* (Erin, Ont.: The Porcupine's Quill, 1981), p. 10.

31. Dale Zieroth, "Birth," *Mid-River* (Toronto: Anansi, 1981), pp. 14-15.

CHAPTER EIGHT: A PLAY BOX
FULL OF PLAYS

Epigraphs: James Reaney, "Production Notes: 1966," *Listen to the Wind* (Vancouver: Talonbooks, 1972), p. 117; Barbara Herrnstein Smith, *On the Margins of Discourse: The Relation of Literature to Language* (Chicago: Univ. of Chicago Press, 1978), p. 132

1. For a summary of the mythical implications of the child figure in Reaney's work, see Terry Griggs, "James Reaney's Giants," *Essays on Canadian Writing* 24-25 (Winter-Spring 1982 -83): 15-31.

2. James Reaney, "Play-box," *Selected Shorter Poems*, ed. Germaine Warkentin (Erin, Ont.: Press Porcépic, 1975), p. 12.

3. James Reaney, "Ten Years at Play," *Dramatists in Canada: Selected Essays*, ed. W.H. New (Vancouver: Univ. of British Columbia Press, 1972), p. 78.

4. James Reaney, *Colours in the Dark* (1969; rpt. Vancouver: Talonbooks, 1975), pp. 16, 70. Subsequent references are to this edition.

5. Ronald Huebert, "James Reaney: Poet and Dramatist," *Canadian Theatre Review* 13 (Winter 1977): 126.

6. G.D. Parker, "The key word . . . is 'listen': James Reaney's sonic environment," *Mosaic* 14:4 (Fall 1981): 8.

7. It is worth remembering, here, that Piaget's term "egocentrism" not does connote selfishness. Maurice Merleau-Ponty's clarification seems a helpful description of the processes of understanding evoked in *Colours in the Dark*:

Since the primordial *me* is virtual or latent, egocentrism is not at all the attitude of a *me* that expressly grasps itself (as the term "egocentrism" might lead us to believe). Rather, it is the attitude of a *me* which is unaware of itself and lives as easily in others as it does in itself—but which, being unaware of others in their own separateness as well, is in truth is no more conscious of them than of itself.

See "The Child's Relation with Others" in *The Primacy of Perception and other Essays on Phenomenological Psychology, the Philosophy of Art, History and Politics*, ed. James M. Edie (Evanston, IL: Northwestern Univ. Press, 1964), p. 119.

8. Cited in Allison J. Elliot, *Child Language* (Cambridge, Eng.: Cambridge University Press, 1981), p. 40.

9. J. Stewart Reaney, *James Reaney* (Toronto: Gage, 1977), p. 16.

10. Cf. Richard N. Coe, "On Being Very, Very Surprised . . . Eugène Ionesco and the Vision of Childhood" in *The Dream and the Play: Ionesco's Theatrical Quest*, ed. Moshe Lazar (Malibu, CA: Undena, 1982), pp. 1-19. Coe's discussion of the "inspired anti-logic of the child" and its connection to 'Theatre of the Absurd' is very relevant to Reaney's drama. Also see Coe's consideration of patterns of colour in Ionesco and their connection to the child vision, pp. 12-19.

11. Mavor Moore, *Four Canadian Playwrights* (Toronto: Holt, Rinehart and Winston, 1973), pp. 57-58.

12. James Reaney, "Note," *Apple Butter and Other Plays For Children* (Vancouver: Talonbooks, 1973), p. 101.

13. *Ibid.*, p. 105.

14. Iona and Peter Opie, *The Lore and Language of Schoolchildren* (Oxford: Clarendon Press, 1959). For a general description, see pp. 1-16.

15. Louis Dudek, "A Problem of Meaning," *Canadian Literature* 59 (Winter 1974): 20-21.

16. See, on sectarian rhymes, Opie and Opie, *Lore*, p. 345.

17. James Reaney, "First Letter: To the Avon River above Stratford, Canada," *Twelve Letters to a Small Town* in *Selected Longer Poems*, ed. Germaine Warkentin (Erin, Ont.: Press Porcépic, 1976), p. 39. For a valuable account of

the pattern of development in this important poem, including several interesting comments on the child's language, see Colin Browne, "Reaney's *Twelve Letters*: A Portrait of the Artist as a Young Boy," *Essays on Canadian Writing* 24-25 (Winter-Spring 1982 -83): 100-29.

18. Reaney, "The Killdeer," *Selected Shorter Poems*, p. 77.
19. Alvin Lee, *James Reaney* (New York: Twayne, 1969), p. 157.
20. *Ibid.*, p. 159.

CHAPTER NINE: CHILD, MAGICIAN, POET

Epigraph: Daniel G. Hoffman, "In the Beginning," *Norton Introduction to Literature: Combined Shorter Edition*, eds. Carl E. Bain, Jerome Beaty, and J. Paul Hunter (New York: W. W. Norton, 1973), pp. 1147; "Portrait of the Autist as a New World Driver," *The Collins Book of Australian Poetry*, ed. Rodney Hall (Sydney: Collins, 1981), p. 340.

1. Dennis Lee, "Roots and Play: Writing as a 35-Year-Old Children," *Canadian Children's Literature* 4 (1976): 29.
2. Michael Holquist, "What is a Boojum? Nonsense and Modernism" (1969), in Lewis Carroll, *Alice in Wonderland*, ed. Donald J. Gray, Norton Critical Edition (New York: W.W. Norton, 1971), p. 404.
3. Elizabeth Sewell, "The Balance of Brillig," in *Alice*, Norton Critical Edition, p. 377.
4. Holquist, "What is a Boojum?", p. 409.
5. Dennis Lee, *Alligator Pie* (Toronto: Macmillan, 1974), p. 32. Further quotations are from this edition. For a discussion of the appeal of Lee's *Nicholas Knock and Other People* for children, see Perry Nodelman, "The Silver Honkabeast: Children and the Meaning of Childhood," *Canadian Children's Literature* 12 (1978): 26-34.
6. Lee, "Roots and Play," p. 45.
7. *Ibid.*, p. 35.
8. Lee, *Alligator Pie*, p. 63.
9. Julia Kristeva, *Desire in Language: A Semiotic Approach to Literature and Art*, ed. Leon S. Roudiez, trans. Thomas Gora, Alice Jardine and Leon S. Roudiez (New York: Columbia Univ. Press, 1980), p. 133.
10. *Ibid.*, p. 134.
11. Lee, "Roots and Play," p. 50. The standard metrical pattern of the nursery rhyme "is the 4 x 4 duple stanza which makes free use of initial offbeats and unrealised beats," Derek Attridge, *The Rhythms of English Poetry* (London: Longman, 1982), p. 341. The phrase "alligator pie," which has three accents in conventional scansion, has only two in the nursery rhyme bounce.
12. Natalie Waterson, "Evidence for Non-Segmental, Whole-Pattern Speech Perception and Production from a Child's First Recitations of Nursery Rhymes," *Proceedings of the Second International Congress for the Study of Child Language*, II, eds Carol Thew and Carolyn Johnson (Lanham, MD: Univ. Press of America, 1984), pp. 57-72. Nursery rhyme as a form, or language, for expressing the child's perception has attracted surprisingly little critical attention. One minor exception is the discussion of the tension between adult theme and child's form in Eleanor Risteen Gordon, "Daddy, Mummy and Stevie: The Child-Guise in Stevie Smith's Poetry," *Modern Poetry Studies* 11: 3 (1983): 232-44.
13. Dwight Bolinger, *Aspects of Language*, 2nd ed. (New York: Harcourt Brace Jovanovich, 1975), p. 6.
14. Peter A. and Jill G. de Villiers, *Early Language*, (Cambridge, MA.: Harvard Univ. Press, 1979), p. 26.
15. Alison J. Elliot, *Child Language* (Cambridge, Eng.: Cambridge Univ. Press, 1981), pp. 151-52.
16. *Ibid.*, p. 41.
17. Sewell, "The Ballance of Brillig," pp. 384-85.
18. A good summary of the research on children and metaphor is found in Andrew Ortony, Ralph E. Reynolds and Judith A. Arter, "Metaphor: Theoretical and Empirical Research," *Psychological Bulletin* 85: 5 (September 1978): 919-43. This article generally supports a conclusion by Matter and Davis (1975): "In early stages of language acquisition children produce categorical errors and mistakes that can be taken as metaphorical expression but

are not" (p. 931). See also Nancy Budwig, Michael Bamberg and Amy Strage, "A Case for Literal Metaphor in Child Language," *Proceedings of the Second International Congress for the Study of Child Language*, II, eds. Carol Thew and Carolyn Johnson, (Lanham, MD: Univ. Press of America, 1984) pp. 112-26. Although this article argues that metaphor is inherent in any process of constructing reality, the term "literal" still suggests a distinctive form of metaphor dominant in child language.

19. Ortony *et al.*, "Metaphor," p. 927.
20. bill bissett, *Selected Poems: Beyond Even Faithful Legends* (Vancouver: Talonbooks, 1980), p. 46. Unless otherwide identified, further quotations are from this edition.
21. Ruth Hirsch Weir, *Language in the Crib* (The Hague: Mouton, 1962), pp. 150-51. Weir's analysis of pre-sleep monologues is very interesting. Of special interest for this chapter is her discussion of "the selection of a grammatical pattern where substitution occurs in one slot of the grammatical frame," p. 109.

The child has been the almost inevitable patron saint of the avant-garde in the last two centuries. As Reinhard Kuhn notes of a poem published by Clemens Bretano in 1800: "[the child's] incoherent babbling forms the basis of a far more precious orison." (*Corruption in Paradise*, p. 202). Lionel Trilling laments the avant garde's "preference for the infinite unexercised potential of infancy over the lonely and limited freedom available to adult enterprises" (cited in Alan Williamson, *Introspection and Contemporary Poetry*, Cambridge, MA: Harvard Univ. Press, 1984, p. 106). W. Bliem Kern's manifesto of 1973 could be bissett's: "I am exploring the oral world of nonlinear phenomena, the innerspeech, the dialogues as a child before I learned the signs and symbols of our language" (Richard Kostelanetz, *The Old Poetries and the New*, Ann Arbor: Univ. of Michigan Press, 1981, p. 204).
22. Cf. Marie-Louise von Franz, *Puer Aeternus*, 2d ed. (1970; rpt. Santa Monica, CA: Sigo Press, 1981). Although I do not have the expertise to argue that this Jungian analysis does or does not describe bissett, I find that many aspects of von Franz's description of the type—the "fear of being pinned down," the naïveté and spontaneity which is "close to being something worthless," and especially the interpretation of drawings and verbal questioning in St. Exupéry's *The Little Prince*—help to describe the complexity of bissett's simplicity. Pp. 2, 59, 10-21.

23. Kristeva, *Desire in Language*, p. 142. Stephen Scobie also cites Kristeva in pointing to connections between early childhood speech and post-modern experiments in poetry. See his *bpNichol: What History Teaches* (Vancouver: Talonbooks, 1984), especially pp. 25-26, 47-48, and 68.
24. bill bissett, *(th) Gossamer Bed Pan* (1967; rpt. Vancouver: blewointment, 1974).
25. de Villiers, *Early Language*, p. 23.
26. Peter D. Eimas, "The Perception of Speech in Early Infancy," *Scientific American* 252: 1 (January 1985): 52. Eimas is summarizing research by Janet F. Werker and Richard C. Tees.
27. Len Early, "Introduction," bill bissett, *Selected Poems*, p. 15.
28. See, e.g., bill bissett, "heart/flash/us," *Sailor* (Vancouver: Talonboooks, 1978), unpaginated.
29. bill bissett, "what duz an exchange look like" *Medicine My Mouth's On Fire* (Ottawa: Oberon, 1974), unpaginated.
30. Elliot, *Child Language*, pp. 39-40.
31. Guy R. Lefrançois, *Of Children: An Introduction to Child Development* (Belmont, CA: Wadsworth, 1973), p. 263.
32. Elliot, *Child Language*, p. 138.
33. de Villiers, *Early Language*, p. 71.
34. Elliot, *Child Language*, p. 145.
35. de Villiers, *Early Language*, p. 37.
36. Ortony et al., "Metaphor," p. 927.
37. Kristeva, *Desire and Language*, pp. 142-43. See also Bernie Selinger, "*Gulliver's Travels*: Swift's Version of Identity Formation," *Mosaic* 17: 3 (Summer 1984): 1-16. Selinger argues that a work often remembered for "stink and excrement" might be better understood through attention to "the first stage of child development," and a link between infant language, nonsense, and satire.
38. Barbara Herrnstein Smith, *On the Margins of Discourse: The Relation of Literature to Language* (Chicago: Univ. of Chicago Press, 1978), pp. 130-31.
39. Smith, *Margins*, p. 131.
40. de Villiers, *Early Language*, p. 73.

AFTER WORDS

Epigraph: Ron Smith, "Nicole: August 20" in *Seasonal* (Victoria: Sono Nis, 1984), p. 29.

INDEX

All authors mentioned in the text are cited. Titles of individual works are given separate entries only where reference to the particular work is more than incidental. Principal references are shown in bold face.